You and Your Pension

ALSO AVAILABLE:

ACTION FOR A CHANGE: *A Student's Guide to Public Interest Organizing* (second edition, 1972), by Ralph Nader and Donald Ross

THE CHEMICAL FEAST: *Ralph Nader's Study Group Report on the Food and Drug Administration*, by James S. Turner

THE CLOSED ENTERPRISE SYSTEM: *Ralph Nader's Study Group Report on Antitrust Enforcement*, by Mark J. Green with Beverly C. Moore, Jr., and Bruce Wasserstein

THE COMPANY STATE: *Ralph Nader's Study Group Report on DuPont in Delaware*, by James Phelan and Robert Pozen

THE INTERSTATE COMMERCE OMISSION: *Ralph Nader's Study Group Report on the Interstate Commerce Commission and Transportation*, by Robert C. Fellmeth

OLD AGE: THE LAST SEGREGATION: *Ralph Nader's Study Group Report on Nursing Homes*, Claire Townsend, Project Director

POLITICS OF LAND: *Ralph Nader's Study Group Report on Land Use in California*, Robert C. Fellmeth, Project Director

SMALL—ON SAFETY: *The Designed-in Dangers of the Volkswagen*, by the Center for Auto Safety

SOWING THE WIND: *A Report for Ralph Nader's Center for Study of Responsive Law on Food Safety and the Chemical Harvest*, by Harrison Wellford

UNSAFE AT ANY SPEED: *The Designed-in Dangers of the American Automobile* (expanded and updated, 1972), by Ralph Nader

VANISHING AIR: *Ralph Nader's Study Group Report on Air Pollution*, by John C. Esposito

THE WATER LORDS: *Ralph Nader's Study Group Report on Industry and Environmental Crisis in Savannah, Georgia*, by James M. Fallows

WATER WASTELAND: *Ralph Nader's Study Group Report on Water Pollution*, by David Zwick with Marcy Benstock

WHAT TO DO WITH YOUR BAD CAR: *An Action Manual for Lemon Owners*, by Ralph Nader, Lowell Dodge, and Ralf Hotchkiss

WHISTLE BLOWING: *The Report of the Conference on Professional Responsibility*, edited by Ralph Nader, Peter Petkas, and Kate Blackwell

THE WORKERS: *Portraits of Nine American Jobholders*, by Kenneth Lasson

SUPERIOR PUBLIC LIBRARY
331.25 N125y
Nader, Ralph.
You and your pension

3 6120 00047 6493

WITHDRAWN

Founded in 1888

NH

You and Your Pension

Ralph Nader and Kate Blackwell

GROSSMAN PUBLISHERS, NEW YORK 1973

331.25
N125y

Copyright © 1973 by Ralph Nader

All rights reserved

First published in 1973 in a hardbound and
paperbound edition by Grossman Publishers
625 Madison Avenue, New York, N.Y. 10022

Published simultaneously in Canada by
Fitzhenry and Whiteside, Ltd.

SBN 670-79390-6 (hardbound)
670-79391-4 (paperbound)

Library of Congress Catalogue Card Number: 72-81084

Printed in U.S.A.

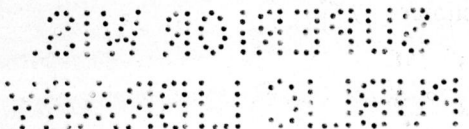

CONTENTS

I.	Introduction	1
II.	The Promise to Pay	4
III.	Pension Stakes	12
IV.	Rules of the Game	19
V.	Hedging the Bet	30
VI.	Playing Against the Economy	45
VII.	Winner Take Nothing	57
VIII.	The Dealers	65
IX.	The Payoff	79
X.	The Public Stake	92
XI.	Revising the Rules	108
XII.	Your Turn to Play	127
	Appendices	147
	Notes	198
	Index	209

ACKNOWLEDGMENT

This book could not have been written without the help of Karen Ferguson, attorney with the Public Interest Research Group of Washington, D.C., whose knowledge of the complicated subject of pensions and attention to detail was invaluable to the authors. We also gratefully acknowledge the assistance of PIRG attorney Helena Bargholtz.

You and Your Pension

I

Introduction

This book was written for one reason: millions of the people—possibly many more than half—who expect pensions never get them. While this fact has long been recognized by employers, union leaders, pension managers, government officials, lawyers, and economists, the individual employee who loses out is bitterly disappointed. Few expectant pensioners realize that their interest in a reliable pension is compromised by a web of other conflicting interests—the employer's interest in holding down costs and retaining control of the plan's operation, the union's interest in larger benefits regardless of how few get them, among others.

Although private pensions have been discussed in Congress and the Federal government for years, most of the information that has been gathered at this level has never filtered down to those who are most concerned—the potential beneficiaries of private pensions. Most people who expect to get a pension are unaware of the crucial difference between the pension fund's promise to pay and the multitude of strings attached to the promise. Most people plan on that pension for retirement security and never know that pensions are no more certain than horseraces.

The aim of this book is to draw the attention of the millions of employees enrolled in private pension plans to the risks they take when they bet on a payoff from private pensions. Awareness is a first step toward reducing these risks.

This is not to say that all expectant pensioners are placidly accepting their lot. Many are unhappy with the conditions they must meet to get a pension or dissatisfied with their lack of influence on how their plans are run. We solicited the opinions of more than 800 people who had indicated their interest by writing to us, to Federal agencies, or to congressmen. We received responses from over 500. Half were active workers who are enrolled or have been enrolled in private pension plans; the others were retired employees, many of whom have lost their benefits or received reduced benefits. Their responses indicate that employees are deeply concerned about the role of pensions in their retirement security. In the following pages, we report their views on various aspects of the private pension system as it affects the supposed beneficiaries.

The public has a great stake in a private pension system that offers greater reliability and broader coverage than what exists now. As Professor Dan McGill has pointed out: ". . . private pension plans have become more than an instrument of business (and union) policy; they are now an imposing instrument of social policy. In a very real sense the business community and the federal government have become partners in *a vast program designed to provide economic security in old age.* This goal will be achieved by one route or the other. To the extent that the private approach falls short of its potential, greater reliance will have to be placed on the public approach."[1] Americans are already supporting the private pension system with a three billion dollar annual tax subsidy. Beyond the overt cost are enormous but less obvious economic effects, including private pensions' tendency to reduce labor mobility and the impact of pension fund investment policies on our economic priorities. Senator Jacob Javits has noted that private pension funds, with assets currently of 152.8 billion dollars, represent "the largest concentration of wealth with the least regulation in the country." People must ask whether the performance of private pensions justifies this latitude and the consequent opportunities for misuse. They must also ask whether private pensions justify their not inconsiderable social costs by meeting the needs of those whom they purport to serve.

With increasing recognition that the system excludes a substantial part of the private work force, that it fails to pay benefits to millions who are covered by it, and that the money belonging to workers can be and is flagrantly misused, proposals for reform have been put forward. But if and when changes are made in the private pension system, through legislation or "voluntary" action on the part of the pension industry, will they reflect the needs and desires of beneficiaries? Too often the potential recipients of pensions are absent from the legislative debates and are discussed as if they were abstract quantities.

What follows is an attempt to help the 34 million men and women enrolled in private pension plans join the debate and exercise influence over pensions on which they, above all others, have the most pressing claim.

II

The Promise to Pay

Charlie Reed thought he was going to get a pension. He went to work when he was twenty-one as a coal miner for Jones & Laughlin Steel Corporation, and after twenty-three years in the mines, he was laid off. He waited for a recall, but none came. Numbers of small mines were closing under the pressures of mechanization, and thousands of miners were looking for work wherever they could find it. Like many others, Reed finally found a job outside the coal industry to keep him and his family going.

Thirteen years later, Reed applied for the pension he thought he had been earning during his twenty-three years in the mines. He found there wasn't one; instead, there was a rule Reed didn't know about: he had to have twenty years of service *within the thirty years preceding his application for benefits.* The rules made no exception for miners who had been laid off.

Reed was incensed. He began looking for other miners in southwestern Pennsylvania who had worked for at least twenty years and then found they weren't eligible for pensions when they retired. He has found 1200 of them.[1]

The pension plan booklet that told Reed he would receive a pension said nothing about the possibility that he might be laid off, or that eligibility rules would disqualify him, or that new technology would leave thousands in the industry without jobs or pensions. Your pension description probably doesn't deal with such possibilities either, but they exist in every line of work for every employee who is counting on getting a pension someday.

Approximately 34 million wage and salary workers are relying on the private pension's promise of retirement income. It is an important promise. For most people it means the difference between poverty and a modestly adequate standard of living after they retire. But implicit in the fine print of the private pension system is the probability that *at least half the people covered by pensions will never collect a penny.*

In fact, nobody even knows exactly how many people who expect pensions end up getting them. One out of two is probably the most optimistic guess. But many people believe that figure is too high. Senator Jacob Javits estimates that pension benefits go to as few as one of twelve—certainly not much more than one of ten—covered employees.[2] The Western Conference of Teamsters says that only one of six employees who enroll in the union's pension plan collects a benefit.[3] A study of pension plans in ten low-wage industries covering 60,000 workers found that only one of ten employees could expect to receive a pension.[4]

Most people who enroll in pension plans don't hear about odds; they hear promises. This is especially true in the early work years, when retirement seems a long way off. Then you are probably content with what the pension managers tell you will happen. As the years go by, your pension becomes more important; you're getting older and you see that you're not able to save very much. You have the children's education and the house to pay for, and everything costs more every year. You feel better when you remember what the pension booklet told you about the benefits waiting for you at sixty-five. You may hear about other employees who don't find a pension waiting for them at retirement, but it's easy to forget about the losers. You're a steady worker; you've been with the company a long time. It can't happen to you.

If you are inclined to say, "It can't happen to me," meet some of the people who found out it could. They aren't merely the short-term employees who quit after a couple of years or jumped from job to job; many have worked thirty years or more, often for the same company. In fact, many of them are exactly the people you thought pensions were set up to help. Most of them thought so, too.

James Tyler, a construction worker from Lakewood, California, paid his union dues for thirty-one years. He worked under the same union local for a number of years and then was told that in order to take a job six miles from his home, he had to join another local. He did. Later, when he applied for a pension, he found he wasn't eligible. After thirty-one years in the same industry, he didn't have enough years of continuous service under either local.

He didn't know that *you may not get a pension if you change unions or even union locals.*

Joseph Mintz, fifty-six, of Buena Park, California, has been in aerospace work for over thirty years and has no pension coming to him. For twenty-seven years he worked for three different companies. At each job, he was laid off before he had the ten-year minimum service requirement for a pension. One company laid him off after nine years and ten months. He always got another job, but not a pension.

He didn't know that *you may not get a pension if you are laid off or change jobs.*

A glass worker was employed for thirty-two years by the same company in Salem, New Jersey. When he was forty-eight, he had a stroke and was forced to quit work. He never received a pension: he had to reach age fifty before he was eligible.

He didn't know that *you may not get a pension if you become disabled before a certain age.*

A foundry worker in Cleveland, Ohio, was fifty-one and had worked for the same employer for twenty-one years when the company closed down. By that time, the worker had contracted emphysema and was partially disabled, with little chance for another job. He found he didn't have a chance for a pension either. When the plant closed, the pension plan was terminated without enough money to pay him even part of the benefit he had earned.

He didn't know that *you may not get a pension if your company goes out of business or if the plan terminates for any other reason.*

Harry Oakes of St. Paul, Minnesota, worked for a large department store for fifty-two years before he retired at the age of sixty-six. He received his pension benefit for thirteen months. Then the company went bankrupt and the pension fund—including payments to retirees—was terminated.

He didn't know that *you may lose your benefits sometime after you retire if the pension fund terminates.*

Although thousands lose their benefits every year, almost nobody expects to. Many employees have no idea of the conditions they must meet to get a pension. Some have forfeited their pension rights many years before they retire, but don't find out until they apply for benefits. One woman worked in the same industry and belonged to the same union local for twenty-six years. The only break was a five-year period when paralysis of her arm and fingers, the result of an industrial accident, forced her to work at another job. After she recovered, she returned to her former job and worked for nine years.

"I was reinstated as a union member in good standing, and I was never told that I had forfeited my status in any way," she wrote. But when she applied for a pension, she was turned down. The rules said you had to have twenty *consecutive* years of employment.[5]

Ignorance of the rules occurs not only among lower-level employees. One man who quit his job of eighteen years to go with another company was confident he would keep his pension rights because he had completed fifteen years with the company and was older than forty-five, as stipulated in the plan eligibility rules. But after he left, his former employer pointed out the fine print and cancelled his pension rights because he had gone to work for a company that was considered a competitor. This man had been his company's personnel manager—the person in charge of explaining the pension plan to other employees.[6]

The manner in which plans are presented encourages a false sense of security. For example, plan booklets given to employees often imply that an employee has a separate account that cannot be touched. They may say, for example, that contributions will be made for each employee and leave the impression that separate contributions are made rather than a lump sum payment based on a percentage of the payroll, as is usually the case. Actually, the monies in most pension funds are *not* allocated to specific individuals. Furthermore—a point even fewer people realize—the money in the fund generally amounts to considerably *less* than the benefits promised to plan participants. If all the claims had to be paid off today, it is doubtful that your plan would have enough money to meet them.

Most pension plans are "underfunded," and when the demand exceeds what is there, benefits have to be cut. That is what happened when the Studebaker plant in South Bend, Indiana, closed in 1964 leaving most of the 8500 employees without pensions or with reduced pensions, because there wasn't enough in the fund. Only employees who were sixty or older and had at least ten years of service got their full benefits. Those between forty and fifty-nine with ten years of service got 15 percent of their promised benefits; everyone else got nothing. One fifty-nine-year-old employee who had worked for the company since he was sixteen ended up with only 15 cents for every dollar of pension he thought he was earning during those years.

Because most plans are registered with the Internal Revenue Service (this is how employers obtain a tax deduction on the money they invest in the pension plan), many people believe that the soundness of their plans is guaranteed. Studebaker illustrates the fact that they are not. No government regulation requires an employer to contribute enough money to cover all claims. Nor is there any guarantee that your employer will continue to fund the pension plan at all. Except under certain union-negotiated plans, employers usually reserve the right to alter, modify, or terminate the plan at any time.[7] Another clause in the pension contract may give the employer the right to suspend, reduce, or discontinue contributions at any time—if business is falling off, for example, or if profits are down. No government regulation requires an employer to continue a plan. All an employer is required to do is pay out all the funds to employees when the plan is terminated. An employer is not responsible for claims that cannot be met because the pension fund does not have enough money.

Furthermore, employees have little protection when their pension funds are lost or mismanaged. Former Secretary of Labor George P. Shultz has said that in most cases of abuse and self-dealing by pension fund managers, uncovered by the Labor Department, plan participants were helpless to defend themselves. "It is disturbing that in virtually none of these cases was effective action taken by plan participants or beneficiaries or Federal authorities," Shultz told a congressional committee.[8]

As private pension plans are set up today, your security—the promise that the pension plan will pay—is only one of the considerations that go into formulation and operation of the plan. That objective often conflicts with the interests of the employer or the union or both. When decisions are made on how a plan will be operated, trade-offs are made—and the promise to pay is inevitably weakened in the process. The right to a pension at an early age may be traded off for larger benefits for a few long-time employees. Contributions to cover all or most claims on the plan may be traded off in favor of keeping costs down and benefits up.[9] Union leaders and employers rarely bother to explain these considerations to the potential beneficiaries.

Of all groups with an interest in private pensions, the intended beneficiaries are the least informed and have the least influence on the operation of the plan. It's not surprising that their interests usually get the worst of the trade-offs.

In view of all the conditions surrounding your pension, it is hard to imagine how a throw of the dice would involve much greater risk than staking your retirement on the private pension system. As one former government official has put it: "In all too many cases the pension promise shrinks to this: 'If you remain in good health and stay with the same company until you are sixty-five years old, and if the company is still in business, and if your department has not been abolished, and if you haven't been laid off for too long a period, and if there's enough money in the fund, and if that money has been prudently managed, you will get a pension!' " [10]

Professor Merton C. Bernstein has put it another way: "The losses of many provide the funds with which the payoff is made to the lucky few—just as at any honest race track." [11]

So the first lesson for you to remember about pensions is that they are a gamble you could easily lose. The following chapters will help you judge the odds on your chances for receiving a benefit. They will outline the hazards and suggest ways in which you may be able to prevent loss of pension or pension credits. In some cases, you may be able to protect your pension rights by finding out the conditions you have to meet to get one. In other cases, you and your fellow employees may be able to influence the union or your employer to make certain changes in the pension plan to give you more security. If pressures at the local level fail, you can support and urge passage of Federal legislation to require private pension managers to give you more security. At the very least, you don't have to be taken by surprise if you have no pension when you retire—as happens to so many people—and you may be able to make other provisions for your retirement. It is best to be wary. For in the long run, you would have to be an economist, a financial wizard, a labor expert, and Jimmy the Greek rolled into one to come up with a sure prediction.

III

Pension Stakes

People don't enroll in pension plans in the same way they would put their money on a horse or buy a lottery ticket: gamblers know they are taking a chance; most employees who work under pension plans count on getting them, because a pension plan, as they see it, is part of their wages and because pensions make the difference between a comfortable old age and years of poverty and deprivation.

Most employees believe that money paid into the pension fund by their employer is theirs because they earned it. The great majority of the people who answered our questionnaire said that they would describe pensions as wages earned by employees rather than gifts from employers. (For tabulation of questionnaires see Appendix A.)

Mrs. Jane Bradshaw of Battle Creek, Michigan, voiced the

sentiments of most people who wrote to us. Mrs. Bradshaw had been retired and receiving a pension for two years when her former company went out of business. Because there was too little money in the fund to pay off all claims, the fund management cut pensioners' benefits by 28 percent. Mrs. Bradshaw wrote: "I feel that my pension was my security and I had earned it and I do not think it was right to cut it after I had been retired for two years. . . . My pension is part of my livelihood and I need it. I do not want to become a charity case when I feel that this is rightfully mine and that I have earned it."

Pensions are a crucial insurance for retirement since Social Security benefits alone are never adequate, paying only about one-third the amount a worker earns before he retires.[1] The average Social Security benefit for retired workers in December 1971 was only $132 a month. For widows, the average monthly payment was only $113.[2] Yet the government estimates that most retired couples—all those living in an urban area—need a minimum of $241 a month for a subsistence standard of living.[3]

But the need of millions of American workers for security in retirement has been only one of the underlying reasons for the rise of the private pension system—and often a minor one. The major purpose of the earliest pension plans was to help employers replace older workers without simply turning them out in the cold. Pensions were recognized as good business because they were less expensive than keeping unproductive employees on the payroll.[4] They were also valued by employers, and have continued to be, as a means of retaining good employees for long periods and reducing costly turnover in the work force. (Even union leaders have tended to assess pensions from a narrow point of view, looking upon them as an instrument to keep the union strong rather than for their advantages to the wage-earner.)

Under the earliest pension plans, benefits were usually paid from company operating funds, and employers were careful to present pensions as gratuities or rewards for long and faithful service, rather than rights the employees earned. One of the earliest plans stated: "This Pension Plan is a voluntary act on the part of the company and is not to be deemed or construed to be a part of any contract of employment, or as giving any employee any enforcible right against the Company. The Board of Directors of the Company reserves the right to alter, amend or annul or cancel the plan or any part of it at any time. The right of the Company to discharge any employee at any time shall not be affected by this plan, nor shall such employee have any interest in any pension after discharge." [5]

Even though the concept of private pensions has radically changed since this plan was drawn up, most company plans still contain many of the provisions found in the earliest plans: generally, the company may "alter, amend or annul or cancel the plan or any part of it at any time"; employees are denied enforcible rights against the company to gain their pensions; and employees may be fired even though it means losing their pensions.

In the early years of pensions, a few labor unions—notably the craft and railroad unions, where job turnover was traditionally low—began to create their own pension funds for their members. One of the earliest, the Granite Cutters retirement fund, established in 1905, required that would-be pensioners be at least sixty-two when they retired, and have spent twenty-five years in the union; it paid $60 a year in benefits. Although average benefits are higher now, the requirements for getting them are not substantially changed; in many plans workers must still work many years and reach retirement age before gaining pension rights.

Under the early union plans, members contributed directly from their own pockets, employers made no contributions. In 1927, the American Federation of Labor, which had initially opposed employer-financed plans as paternalistic and a threat to unionization, began to campaign for retirement plans supported by employers.[6] Today only one percent of all covered workers are in plans fully financed by employees. The rest are in plans supported wholly or in large part by employers; only about one out of four covered workers contribute to their pensions. Almost all collectively bargained plans are financed entirely by specified employer contributions, and employees contribute nothing.

In the 1920's insurance companies began selling group annuities to employers for their workers' pensions. These insured pension plans became especially popular among employers after passage of the Social Security Act in 1935 as supplements to Social Security benefits.

Between 1900 and 1940 the growth of private pensions was slow. By 1940 about 4 million people were covered.[7] But after World War II private pension plans suddenly began to boom, not because employers were suddenly more concerned about the retirement security of workers, but because they were competing for workers in a tight civilian labor market.[8] Under the postwar restrictions on wages, pensions were a good device to attract and hold employees because they were exempt from the legal limitations on cash-wage raises. In addition, they offered employers a way to avoid the tax on excess profits. And since employers' contributions to pension plans were tax-deductible under a 1926 law, "the net cost to employers was decidedly less than the actual contributions to the plans."[9]

Unions also began to press employers for pensions as fringe benefits in lieu of cash-wage increases. Unions argued for pensions partly in the belief that employers would press for higher Social Security benefits in order to reduce the cost of private pension plans. (In 1940, primary Old Age Survivors Insurance benefits—Social Security—averaged $26 a month.)[10] But far from raising the level of Social Security benefits, pensions have helped keep them down by offering the expectation of another source of income for retired people.

Union pressures for pensions increased after the Inland Steel decision in 1949, when the Supreme Court upheld a ruling by the National Labor Relations Board that pension plans were subject to collective bargaining.[11] That same year the Steel Industry Fact Finding Committee decided against cash-wage raises but recommended an employer-financed pension plan that the United Steelworkers were seeking. The committee said the industry had a social obligation to provide workers with pensions. The Steelworkers' victory encouraged the United Auto Workers Union in its drive for pensions, which began during the 1949 recession and was soon successful. These two large unions led the early battle for employer-financed pension plans and are still the trend-setters in changing and improving private pension plans.[12]

By 1950 the number of persons covered by private plans had reached almost 10 million, more than twice what it had been in 1940. Private pensions became a mass movement during the 1950's, with unions negotiating more plans and putting more pressure on employers to establish plans unilaterally. Negotiated multiemployer plans, covering workers in several companies that have joined together for pension plan coverage, particularly in construction, transportation, trade, and services, opened coverage to millions of workers in smaller firms.

By 1960 the number of covered employees had again doubled, showing 21.1 million enrolled in private pension plans.

The decision that pension plans were a proper issue for collective bargaining also helped change the concept of pensions. Most employers felt then—as many do now—that pensions were gifts, rewards for faithful service. But when pensions become part of a contract agreement, they become not gratuities but part of the wage structure or deferred wages belonging to the worker. Even in plans established unilaterally by the employer, they represent part of the total compensation package with which a company seeks to attract and hold a labor force. However, the terms of the pension contract under many pension plans fail to reflect this change in concept, largely because employers and unions have continued to view pensions in the light of their own interests rather than from the beneficiaries' point of view.

Labor unions, though encouraging the concept of private pensions as deferred wages rather than gratuities, have not always followed through by insisting on provisions that would insure workers of getting their deferred wages. Many unions continue to prefer higher benefits for a small number of long-time workers and to resist reforms that would give pensions to more workers, possibly at a reduced level of benefits. Thus the Teamsters Union, whose plans require members to work for twenty years to receive any pension benefits, is not supporting reforms that would require fewer years of service or greater employer contributions. The same is true of the garment unions and others. Unions that exercise significant control over pension funds also tend to oppose greater regulation of pension plans and their monies. The United Mine Workers is a notable example.

Private pensions cannot continue to be justified unless they move beyond employer-union interests to serve the majority of people in the private work force. The following chapters try to pinpoint areas where pensions do not serve employees' interests and suggest what you can do about it. We begin with the broad outlines of the way pensions work.

IV

Rules of the Game

People who lose their benefits commonly ask where "their" money has gone. One man who changed unions after twenty-eight years and lost his pension asked, "What has happened to twenty-eight years of monies paid? Not only for me, but the many hundreds of workers who leave the unions—fattening up their bank accounts." Another disappointed pensioner assumed that "the money they had been putting aside for my retirement, I suppose, reverts back to Lockheed."

In some cases employees are right in assuming that the union or company is getting the benefit of their forfeited pensions (see Chapters V and VI), but much of the confusion and disappointment arise as a result of the difference between what the pension promises and the principle on which it works.

A trucker in Indiana, who found he did not have enough credits for a pension after years in the industry, asked his employer to stop making payments for him into the union pension fund. He assumed that since he wouldn't be allowed to use the money, it would be wasted. He soon received a letter from the chairman of the pension fund explaining: "Even though your application for a pension has been rejected, your employer is obligated to make weekly contributions on all employees covered under their collective bargaining agreement and, therefore, must include you on their monthly remittances."

If the fund administrator had gone on to explain *why* this was true, the worker might have learned one of the basic principles of private pension plans. By and large, pensions work like insurance policies.[1] When you take out fire insurance on your home, your money (insurance premiums) goes into a pool along with the money of other people who are insuring themselves against fire loss. Assume ten people put money into the pool, but only one of the ten loses his home in a fire. He is paid for his loss with money that all ten have paid into the pool. The rest get nothing.

Private pensions do the same thing. Money is paid into the pension fund for *all* enrolled employees. But plans are designed so that benefits are paid only to *some* employees. In the case of the Indiana trucker, money theoretically paid on his behalf by the employer actually would be used to pay benefits to employees who did qualify for a pension.

Many people may be shocked when they realize the principle on which the pension promise is based—and shocked for good reason. After all, there is a good chance that your house will not burn down and you will not need your fire insurance. But all workers, or their beneficiaries, are going to need income at retirement. Keeping this principle in mind, we move on to the nuts and bolts of the pension system.

An employer may himself make the decision to establish a

pension plan or he may arrive at a plan through a bargained agreement with a union; pension plans are divided roughly equally into these two groups. But other factors influence the decision. First, particularly with small businesses, the employer may be approached by a pension "agent," who will try to sell him on the advantages of establishing a pension plan—the kind of plan that the agent's company manages. The agent may be the representative of an insurance company, or a pension consulting firm, or a bank. These pension salesmen are responsible for arousing the interest of many employers in private pension plans. Since pension agents are trying to sell the particular types of plans handled by their companies, they are also instrumental in determining the kind of plan that you are offered.[2]

A second factor affecting the employer's decision to establish a plan is the tax incentive: employers may deduct from their income taxes the amounts they contribute to an employee pension plan, within certain limitations established by the Internal Revenue Service. These tax deductions are important to the employer's decision because they help make it profitable for him to offer you a retirement benefit. (It should also be noted that contributions by employees to their pension plans are not similarly tax deductible.)

The employer also decides what employees he wants to include in the plan. The regulations of the Internal Revenue Service do not grant tax deductions to pension plans that discriminate in favor of executives or any privileged group of employees. (See Chapter VI for instances in which discrimination can occur.) However, tax-exempt plans may be limited to: (1) salaried employees, (2) hourly employees, (3) members of a particular department, (4) union members, (5) nonunion employees, (6) employees with more than the Old Age, Survivors, Disability, and Health Insurance (Social Security) wage base,

(7) employees with more than five years of service, (8) employees who have attained a specified age, or any combination of these groups.[3]

After he has decided what plan he is interested in and what employees it will cover, the employer calls in an actuary to estimate the costs of the plan. A pension actuary is, broadly speaking, someone with special mathematical skills and experience with retirement plans; he may be an employee of an insurance company, or an independent operator, or a member of the employer's own company.

The employer will tell the actuary either the amount of money he wants to contribute to the plan or the kinds of benefits he wants to provide. If he decides on a certain contribution, the actuary will estimate what benefits that money will give employees, under various conditions. This is a very important stage in the development of the pension plan because the money can be divided in many ways depending on the conditions for getting benefits. Remember the pension principle: some forfeit in order that others may gain. Thus, if the employer says he can contribute 5 percent of his annual payroll to the plan, the size of the benefits will depend on how many employees receive them. These conditions are largely arbitrary and can be calculated by the actuary in various ways. The more difficult the conditions are to satisfy—that is, the longer the years of service or the higher the age required—the fewer employees will qualify for pensions, and benefits can be determined accordingly.

If instead the actuary begins his calculations with certain benefit levels, computed either as flat benefits (say $100 a month) or as a percentage of salary (say one percent of compensation for each year of recognized service), he then estimates the cost to the employer of paying the employees those benefits.

Assume that the plan is going to pay employees $100 a month at retirement. Assume also that one hundred employees enter the plan simultaneously at the age of thirty. The actuary estimates that a certain number will not survive until retirement (the mortality rate), a certain number of others will leave the plan before meeting the conditions to qualify for a pension (the withdrawal rate), and a certain number from those who remain will become disabled before qualifying for a benefit (the disability rate). If this leaves only fifty of the original hundred who are expected to receive a benefit, the amount of contributions needed to pay benefits to those who will get them is only half as much as if all one hundred were expected to receive pensions. However, those contributions are usually estimated as a percentage of the payroll going to all one hundred employees, even though half are not expected to receive a pension.

Again the *conditions* for receiving pensions are important. If pensions are to go only to those who stay with the company until retirement, fewer employees can be expected to receive them than if, for example, they could earn some benefits after ten years of service.

Other factors are also taken into account in estimating the cost of the pension plan. Future wage and salary scales must be predicted. Another factor is the interest the monies set aside for pensions will earn: the more they earn, the more the employer's contribution can be reduced. Finally, there are the expenses of operating the plan, which raise its overall cost. These expenses include the fees of lawyers, actuaries, accountants, consultants, investment managers, trustees, and others who play a part in managing the plan.

Since all of these estimates must be made ahead of time, there is a high degree of uncertainty in the expected costs of pension plans. Sometimes the actuary will be wrong, and the cost will prove to be higher than expected; perhaps fewer workers than predicted will die or withdraw from employment; perhaps the earnings of the pension fund are not as high as anticipated. Then there may not be enough money to pay you $100 a month, and your benefit will be reduced—unless the employer agrees to increase his contributions, which is unusual.

There is another reason for uncertainty: the actuary who draws up your plan may not be qualified. It is hardly an exaggeration to say that anyone can call himself an actuary. The profession has no legal status and requires no license. The Internal Revenue Service will accept certifications of cost estimates from any person acceptable to the employer. The report of one expert several years ago is still true: "Unfortunately, some of the persons holding themselves out as actuaries are completely lacking in the technical qualifications and experience needed to provide adequate actuarial guidance." [4] Employers in small and middle-sized firms are especially vulnerable to people of doubtful qualifications when they hire independent consulting actuaries. Large companies often can afford full time actuaries. Since these actuaries have co-responsibilities in addition to the pension plan, large companies tend to be more exacting in finding well-qualified actuaries.

How does the employer pay for the pension plan?

A few plans simply pay benefits, as the claims arise, from the company's operating budget. This pay-as-you-go approach is highly risky for employees, since any financial setback to the company could immediately halt the payment of pension claims, and there would be no monies set aside to pay them. Under "unfunded" pension plans, termination of the plan or bankruptcy of the employer would leave no separate fund for allocation to workers who had earned pensions. Your benefit, under these plans, depends entirely on the future financial strength of your employer and his willingness to meet the obligations of the plan.

Most employers pay for pensions by setting aside monies in a special fund. These are called "funded" pension plans. If the employer decides to fund the pension plan, he must then determine who will manage the money that goes into the fund.

If you are under an "insured" plan, your employer pays his contributions to a life insurance company. (About one-third of all monies paid into private pension funds are handled by insurance companies.) The money may then be used, according to the contract, to buy insurance policies or annuities for qualified employees. Or the money may go into a special account, without being credited to individual employees, which will be used to purchase annuities for employees as they acquire benefit rights.

Most large plans are "noninsured" plans in which the employer's contributions go into a trust fund. (A little less than two-thirds of all monies in private pension funds are in noninsured trust funds.) Again, the money is not credited to you individually. The fund is managed by a trustee or trustees, who may be independent agents, or a bank trust department. The trustee is responsible for investing the monies and paying out benefits to employees as they qualify. Sometimes the trustee will have complete authority to invest the funds. At the other extreme, some pension trust agreements stipulate that the trustee will make only those investments selected by the employer. The employer may, if he wishes, direct the trustee to invest pension funds in his own company, and many employers do so. The trustee has nothing to say about how much money goes into the fund or who gets benefits; these matters are decided by the administrator or pension board, comprised usually of company officers or, in the case of plans managed jointly by employers and unions, of company and union representatives.

Theoretically, the trustee's obligation is to manage the pension fund in the best interest of the beneficiaries. How does he know what your best interest is? Usually he simply decides for himself. Trustees do not consult with beneficiaries about the investment of their funds. There is almost never a provision in a pension trust agreement for an accounting to the employees and pensioners under the plan.[5]

How much money the employer puts into a trust fund or an insurance company to pay for pensions is a decision made entirely by the employer or, in the case of some bargained plans, by the employer and the union together. Most employers will contribute at least enough money each year to cover the pension credits, that is, units of service on which benefits are based, earned by employees during that year. However, when a plan is begun, there is usually a group of employees who have already worked for many years. Most employers want to provide these workers with pensions and give them credit for their past years of service. Thus, when a plan begins, there are already pension credits that must be paid for. Since the problem of paying for "past service credits" is a major reason for loss of pensions, it deserves special attention.

When he starts a plan, an employer could immediately put enough money into the pension fund to cover all past service credits, but this is expensive, and in practice almost no employer does it. An alternative that most employers choose is to put in small amounts of money that will gradually pay for past service credits over a number of years. (The Accounting Principles Board of the American Institute of Certified Public Accountants recommends forty years for funding past service credits.) Some employers will not pay for past service credits at all (all the Internal Revenue Service requires them to do is pay the interest on these past service credits), and if they do not, large amounts of pension credits will not be covered by money in the pension fund. Even if employers put in money gradually to cover these credits, it is usually many years before all credits are paid up.

How, then, are these past service credits paid when an employee retires and qualifies for a pension? Take a worker with ten years of credits earned before the pension plan began. The employer will figure how much he must contribute to pay that worker's benefit when he retires after, say, thirty years of total credited employment. But the employer will have made those contributions only for twenty years—the years after the plan began. He will not contribute the amount that would have been paid during the first ten years, or, at the most, he will contribute only part of that money. When the worker retires, part of the money to pay him his full benefit based on thirty years' employment must come from the contributions nominally made for workers who are not yet retired.

This process of paying benefits may not cause a problem if the pension plan continues to operate. But if it terminates, and all claims must be paid at the same time, the pension fund will not have enough money to pay them all.

If the plan terminates, the employer is not obligated to pay any benefits beyond the monies already contributed to the pension fund. When a plan ends without enough money to pay all claims, the money in the fund must be divided, usually either according to the percentage of the total claims met by the available funds (thus, if the money in the fund covered only half of all the credits earned by workers under the plan, you would get half of your promised benefit) or according to a scale of priorities under which, for example, retired employees and employees beyond the normal retirement age might get all their pension benefits while younger employees with nonforfeitable benefit rights get a certain part of their benefits and employees without nonforfeitable rights get nothing.

As you can see, your employer's promise to pay you a benefit is not as binding as you may have believed. He actually has committed himself to pay the promised benefits *only if money is available in the pension fund.* If for any reason there is not enough money to pay your benefit, your employer is not legally obligated to pay it.

There are several reasons your pension fund may not have enough money to pay your benefit when you retire or if the plan terminates. One is the process of funding past service credits; another could be erroneous estimates of what the plan would cost and what your employer should have been contributing each year to cover all benefit claims. (One economist has noted: "There are no generally accepted standards as to what is meant by the term 'actuarial soundness.' Actuaries of equal skill, experience and judgment can examine the same set of plan specifications and employee data and come up with widely different estimates as to the probable cost of the plan." [6]) Another reason might be that a fund loses money when employment drops off in a declining business and employer contributions, based on compensation to current employees, do not reach the amount anticipated when the plan was set up. Declining profits may prompt an employer to reduce contributions until the fund becomes insolvent, that is, has no money to pay current claims. Except under certain bargained plans that stipulate contributions as part of the employment agreement, your employer may reduce his contributions or alter or amend the terms of the plan in any way.[7] If the fund is not then sufficient to pay your benefit, you cannot hold him responsible: his obligation is limited to paying out money already committed to the fund. Under the terms of almost all company-established plans, he has the right to terminate the plan or to discontinue contributions to it at any time.

It should be noted here that if a plan terminates, any monies that you have contributed as an employee (as distinguished from contributions by your employer) must be returned to you. Some plans, though not all, provide for interest to be paid on employees' contributions. If they do, the interest is usually low (between 2 percent and 3 percent).

These are only the broad outlines of the way private pension plans work, but already you should be able to see some of the risks involved in counting on your pension.

1. Is your plan based on sound "actuarial assumptions"?

2. Is your plan "funded,"—that is, is there a separate fund of money to be used to pay your benefits?

3. Does your employer contribute enough money to the fund to give you some assurance that you will receive a benefit when you retire?

4. If your plan terminates, will it have enough money to cover all claims, and, if not, what percentage of the claims will go unpaid?

5. Who is managing your fund? Is he doing it wisely? Do you know how it is invested?

V

Hedging the Bet

"Dear Mr. Douglas: The Trustees have examined your application for a pension and regret the necessity of advising you that you do not qualify at the present time under the Pension Plan. The reason you do not qualify is as follows:

"LACK OF CREDITS: In order to qualify you must have at least fifteen years of credited service, including two quarters (600 hours) of Future Service. *You do not have a total of fifteen years of credited service.* You have accumulated $11\frac{1}{4}$ years of past service and no future service credits for a total of eleven and one quarter years of credit service only. (Signed) The Board of Trustees."

Thousands of people receive letters like this every year. For many, it is the first they hear about the requirements on which their pensions depend. By the time they find out, it is nearly always too late.

Test yourself. Do you know how many years you must work for your employer to qualify for a pension? Do you know how old you must be? Do you know whether a layoff has wiped out your chance for benefits? Few employers or unions have undertaken the kinds of education programs that might alert workers to the numerous conditions surrounding their pensions.

Many employees could salvage their pensions if they were informed of the conditions they must meet. One man worked sixteen years as a sign painter under pension coverage. After he left his job, he continued as a "dues-paying member in good standing" of the union that operated the pension plan. But later, when he applied for a benefit, he was notified that "I had lost any and all past service credits earned to date because I had not put in a minimum of one hour a year in the sign industry. I told them that I had not been fully and adequately informed about this when I left the industry and tried to explain to them that had I been aware of this rule, common sense would compel me to put in the required one hour a year to retain my pension."

Another man had worked for a manufacturing company in Colorado for twenty-four years when the company shut down the factory. He decided not to accept a job in another facility owned by the same company because he thought his pension was safe: he had worked more than the required twenty years. Later, when he became sixty-five, he contacted the company about his pension. "We were promptly told," he wrote, "that we had no rights, as we had left the company employment prior to reaching age sixty-five. The twenty-four years of constant service did not mean anything."

In both these cases, the employees could have protected their pension rights. This is not always the case. Private pension plans are designed so that many thousands of workers forfeit their benefits because they *cannot* meet the conditions—conditions they have no part in setting and no right to challenge.

How do these conditions operate? A pension plan begins with a certain amount of money. Like slicing a pie, that money can be cut several different ways. It could be cut into large pieces for a few people or smaller pieces for more people.

Take a pension plan that requires you to work under the plan until retirement in order to receive a benefit. That pie is cut so that only a few people share in it; large numbers of people under any plan may be expected to leave before retirement and therefore forfeit their pensions. If the plan gave you a right to a pension after ten years of service, more people would have the opportunity to share in the pension fund.

With these facts in mind, look at your own plan. You run the greatest risk of losing your pension if you are under a plan that gives benefits only to employees who have worked a certain number of years *and* are employed under the plan when they retire. These requirements are found most frequently in multiemployer plans—pension funds contributed to by many employers usually in the same industry and always involving the same union. They are most restrictive when they occur in single-employer plans, where only employment with the company operating the plan counts for a pension.

Most single-employer plans (under which 70 percent of all workers with pension coverage come) allow you to qualify for a benefit at retirement even if you leave the company before you retire. Most also require you to have a certain number of years of service *and* reach a certain age before you qualify. Age requirements can considerably lengthen the requirement for years of service. For example, if you begin work at age twenty-five under a plan that requires fifteen years of service *and* achieving age fifty before you qualify for a pension, you actually have to work for twenty-five years before you are assured of a pension.

Some plans require only years of service to qualify for a pension. The more years required, the more employees will lose benefits. Service requirements are affected, too, by conditions in the industry that cause employees to leave their jobs or be laid off. For example, most companies in the defense industry require ten or fifteen years for vested benefit rights, among the most "liberal" requirements of all pension plans. However, the job turnover in the defense industry is so high that many workers are laid off before they have worked ten years for one company.[1]

Employees are most angered by requirements that say workers must stay with the pension plan until retirement in order to receive a pension. The overwhelming majority of those who responded to our questionnaire said they thought companies or unions should pay benefits to employees even if employees leave their companies or their unions before retirement.

The majority opinion was expressed by the wife of a pensionless sixty-seven-year-old man from New York. She wrote: "What happens to a man who works for twenty-eight years under a union contract that reads you must work to sixty-five years of age to retire [and receive a pension]? At the age of fifty years, you have twenty-eight years in and no security. Then forced by circumstances to join another union for benefits, you find that you're 'too old' to make the required time in a new union for their pension benefits and are left at sixty-seven with NO pension of any kind, only your social security. What has happened to twenty-eight years of monies paid? . . . If a man works hard for twenty or twenty-five years, what difference is it if he is fifty, sixty or seventy? His time is in."

In the past decade many plans have acknowledged this kind of problem by adding so-called vesting provisions.[2] These provisions are those that give you a nonforfeitable right to a pension before you retire. (You won't get the benefit payment, of course, until you retire.) However, the number of workers who are forfeiting their pension credits because they do not meet service or age requirements is still appallingly large. A Senate subcommittee found that in a group of plans where employees had to remain under the plan until retirement or for at least eleven years, only 5 percent of all participants who left the plan during a twenty-year period qualified for a pension. In another group of plans requiring ten or fewer years for qualifying, only 15 percent of the employees who left the plans had attained vested benefit rights.[3]

Members of the private pension industry claim that a majority of covered employees will achieve pensions under present "liberalized" vesting. However, even industry studies show large numbers forfeiting benefits. A study of 864 pension plans by a pension consulting firm found that 34 percent of the participants at the time of the study were not expected to gain benefits from the plans. This is a significant number in itself. Moreover, it does not reflect the *total* loss of benefits because only participants at the time of the study were considered, leaving out those who had already left the plans without benefits.*

Age and service requirements are combined with other conditions that may eliminate even more workers from a share in the pension. In almost all plans, your years of service will count toward a pension only if they are *continuous,* so any break in service can destroy your chance for a pension or reduce your benefit. For example, under the major plans in the steel industry a layoff for two years counts as a break in serv-

---

* The study was made by A. S. Hansen, Inc. and included only plans serviced by the company.[4]

ice and time worked before that is lost for pension eligibility.

Continuous service requirements cost numerous employees their pensions through no fault of their own. Ann Day of Williamsville, New York, worked for an electronics manufacturing company for thirty years. She wrote: "I started with this company in September 1941. I have been laid off periodically for months at a time. The longest period was from May 1966 to May 1968. I now find that all my years of service from 1941 to 1968 do not count toward my retirement because I was off over eighteen months."

Employees rarely have recourse against discharge, even when it means loss of a pension that was only a few years from attainment. The only exception is when a union contract protects union members from discharge without cause. (Even then, cases have been reported where a union refused to back a grievance when a pension was involved.)

Frank Lineberger of Lexington, Kentucky, worked for twenty-six years for the General Telephone Company of Kentucky. He was discharged a little over two years before retirement, at which time he would have received a pension. "I requested, in lieu of release, downgrade to any minor management job or blue-collar job, and further volunteered to transfer to any of the General Telephone Systems in the thirty-four states in which they operate, in order to maintain continuity of employment. This was fruitless. . . . I am presently on unemployment, unable to find work, being age forty-seven, and am planning to go on welfare."

Employees often believe that the reason for their discharge is to save the company from paying them a pension. While this can rarely be proved, there is nothing to prevent an employer from firing a worker just before he or she would qualify for a pension.

Under single-employer plans only service with the company

operating the plan counts toward a pension. Thus discharge by the employer before you qualify for a pension destroys all your pension credits. If you are covered by a multiemployer plan, you can move from job to job within the scope of the plan and carry your credits with you. The scope is usually limited to a single segment of an industry and to a single state. A few plans, such as those operated by the Teamsters Union, cover workers in several industries in a multistate area. But you must be sure, if you change jobs, that your new employer or union local contributes to the same pension plan as your old employer or union local. Otherwise you might find yourself in the position of the worker who wrote: "I have twenty-five years in various union locals and was supposed to get a pension after twenty years continuous [union] membership. I was told I do not qualify because the local I belonged to in Chicago does not contribute to the [Teamsters'] Central States Fund. What happened to all that money my employer paid into the fund for my retirement?"

Employees may also lose pension benefits if they vote for a different union to represent them. The employer is under no obligation to pay benefits except to members of the union that negotiated the pension plan.

In addition, you may lose your pension if you decide to upgrade yourself or take a promotion. B. C. Shore of Newport, Oregon, wrote that "after twenty-five years in the Seafarers International Union, I upgraded myself to a Licensed Officer and joined the Master Mates & Pilots Union (also an A.F. of L. affiliate). Yet I lost all my pension money because they refuse to transfer my credits earned."

Another employee lost his pension when he was promoted within his own company: "I worked for 19 years as an hourly employee, then was transferred to a salaried job [under a different company pension plan]. At the time of my transfer, I was not aware and was not notified that I would lose my 19 years of pension rights. I am still with the same company and in the same plant. When I spoke to management about the unfairness of this, I was told that it 'was just an unfortunate situation.' " [5]

And what of the worker who *wants* to change jobs? He may want to leave a declining industry or low-paying job for higher pay and better opportunities elsewhere. He may have health or family reasons for a job change.

Many workers share the dilemma of the sailor who worked for fifteen years under a multiemployer plan limited to workers on ships. In his early fifties, the sailor developed ulcers and wanted to move to less strenuous work on shore. A well-paid dock job came along, but it was under the jurisdiction of another union. The sailor's choice was between the new job and the loss of fifteen years of pension credits or continuing at a job that endangered his health in order to keep his pension.[6]

Another man had to leave his job in Ohio in order to take his sick wife to Florida. Although he had thirty-five years of continuous service at Universal Cyclops Steel Company in Ohio, he lost all pension benefits because he was only fifty-five years of age. His pension plan made no provision for vesting before retirement at sixty-five.

As one student of pensions has written: "The older worker who loses his job, for one reason or another, after many years of service but before qualifying for a private pension has suffered a retroactive pay cut. The older worker who must forfeit his pension benefit if he chooses to change employers is uncomfortably close to serfdom." [7]

Another condition that may make your service requirements longer is the one that determines when your credited service begins—that is, when you can begin to "participate" in the pension plan. Most plans require that employees work for three to five years and reach age twenty-five before they can begin building credits for a pension. Thus a worker who begins work at nineteen may have to add six years to his minimum service requirement.

If you are older, and about to take a new job, you should be careful to find out whether you can meet the requirements for a pension before you have to retire. In most companies, employees must retire at age sixty-five. If you are fifty-seven and the pension plan requires ten years of service, you won't profit from that plan.

Complicated ways of counting credited service often deprive employees of their pensions, especially when they are not aware of these rules. One employee worked for ten years under a hotel union pension plan. He retired at age sixty-five and applied for a pension. Then the pension manager told him that he had to have worked thirty-five weeks a year for ten years to get a pension. The man wrote: "The last four years [of employment] the chef let me work only thirty-four weeks a year. . . . So I could not get any benefit from the hotel or the union."

Another employee worked for thirty years and then found he was not eligible for a pension because he did not have enough hours per week of credited service. "This," he wrote, "was no fault of mine. They cut my hours below twenty-four hours, which would provide me with all benefits and pension."

Some plans forbid employment with a competitor on pain of losing all pension rights. A personnel manager lost his pension after eighteen years service because of such a condition. Another man resigned from his job and went to work for a competitor six years after such an amendment was added to his plan. The fund's trustees deprived the employee of all his vested rights—including those which he had earned prior to adoption of the rule. The case was taken to court where the three to five years and reach age twenty-five before they can begin building credits for a pension. Thus a worker who begins work at nineteen may have to add six years to his minimum service requirement.

If you are older, and about to take a new job, you should be careful to find out whether you can meet the requirements for a pension before you have to retire. In most companies, employees must retire at age sixty-five. If you are fifty-seven and the pension plan requires ten years of service, you won't profit from that plan.

Complicated ways of counting credited service often deprive employees of their pensions, especially when they are not aware of these rules. One employee worked for ten years under a hotel union pension plan. He retired at age sixty-five and applied for a pension. Then the pension manager told him that he had to have worked thirty-five weeks a year for ten years to get a pension. The man wrote: "The last four years [of employment] the chef let me work only thirty-four weeks a year. . . . So I could not get any benefit from the hotel or the union."

Another employee worked for thirty years and then found he was not eligible for a pension because he did not have enough hours per week of credited service. "This," he wrote, "was no fault of mine. They cut my hours below twenty-four hours, which would provide me with all benefits and pension."

Some plans forbid employment with a competitor on pain of losing all pension rights. A personnel manager lost his pension after eighteen years service because of such a condition. Another man resigned from his job and went to work for a competitor six years after such an amendment was added to his plan. The fund's trustees deprived the employee of all his vested rights—including those which he had earned prior to adoption of the rule. The case was taken to court where the was not aware and was not notified that I would lose my 19 years of pension rights. I am still with the same company and in the same plant. When I spoke to management about the unfairness of this, I was told that it 'was just an unfortunate situation.' " [5]

And what of the worker who *wants* to change jobs? He may want to leave a declining industry or low-paying job for higher pay and better opportunities elsewhere. He may have health or family reasons for a job change.

Many workers share the dilemma of the sailor who worked for fifteen years under a multiemployer plan limited to workers on ships. In his early fifties, the sailor developed ulcers and wanted to move to less strenuous work on shore. A well-paid dock job came along, but it was under the jurisdiction of another union. The sailor's choice was between the new job and the loss of fifteen years of pension credits or continuing at a job that endangered his health in order to keep his pension.[6]

Another man had to leave his job in Ohio in order to take his sick wife to Florida. Although he had thirty-five years of continuous service at Universal Cyclops Steel Company in Ohio, he lost all pension benefits because he was only fifty-five years of age. His pension plan made no provision for vesting before retirement at sixty-five.

As one student of pensions has written: "The older worker who loses his job, for one reason or another, after many years of service but before qualifying for a private pension has suffered a retroactive pay cut. The older worker who must forfeit his pension benefit if he chooses to change employers is uncomfortably close to serfdom." [7]

Another condition that may make your service requirements longer is the one that determines when your credited service begins—that is, when you can begin to "participate" in the pension plan. Most plans require that employees work for man was restored his benefit rights. The court, however, did not rule against the provision but merely found that the language of the amendment clause was not plainly stated.[8]

Some plans also require that retired workers refrain from employment in the industry in order to cut down competition with younger workers. And a few plans try to limit retirement earnings.

Even if you meet all the requirements for a pension, you may lose your benefits if you do not follow certain procedures in applying for it. Many plans require that you make a written application to the plan administrator within a certain period after reaching retirement age, or forfeit your benefit. Some require that an application also be made at the time you leave the plan, if you leave prior to retirement. Many employees forfeit their benefits because they assume that the plan will send them their benefits automatically. Others have difficulty in reaching companies that have relocated, or sold out to another firm, or shut down since they left.

The case of Robert P. O'Hara of Memphis, Tennessee, illustrates the difficulties that can arise: "After twelve years of continuous service, with never taking time off and never being late for work, I was laid off by the Detroit Gasket and Manufacturing Company on August 2, 1962. . . . My Certificate of Vested Rights provides that upon the attainment of age sixty-five, I would be entitled to receive pension equivalent to twelve years. I attained the age of sixty-five on July 10, 1969, at which time I made application for this pension to Mr. Vincent V. Spica, personnel manager of the Gasket Company. He gave me an application form to fill out, sign, and return and promised me in his letter that my application would be processed, after which I would receive the pension effective August 1, 1969.

"After hearing no more from him for six months, I visited

his office and talked to him and was told that their New York attorney had ruled that I was not entitled to the pension. The alibi he offered was that I had failed to make PRELIMINARY application for the pension within thirty days following the date I was laid off! It is true that this is one of the requirements, that TWO separate applications must be made, one within thirty days following layoff date and the other within thirty days of applicant's sixty-fifth birthday. However, I DID make the PRELIMINARY application on August 10, 1962, when I returned to the plant to pick up my final paycheck. I made this preliminary application to Mr. Ken W. Kirk, who preceded Mr. Spica as personnel director. However, Mr. Spica said he had no record of my making this preliminary application in my Service Jacket."

Employees who are denied pensions rarely can find a way to appeal the decision of the plan's trustees. No plans are required to provide appeals channels. Unless a union is willing to take up a case of dismissal that resulted in denial of pension, there is little you can do within the company if you are denied a pension.

Thousands of disappointed employees write to the U.S. Department of Labor each year seeking help in challenging the denial of their pension. Their letters are filed away, and they receive variations of the following form letter in return:

". . . I realize how distressed you must be at the possibility that you may not be able to qualify for pension benefits from this plan after so many years in the industry. However, I know of no way in which the Federal government can intervene on your behalf. Any rights an individual may have to benefits from a private pension plan are governed by the provisions of the plan in which he participates as interpreted by the plan administrator or by the courts as the result of private litigation. No Federal agency has the authority to prescribe or interpret the provisions of private pension plans, to interfere in their internal management, to determine claimant eligibility or to assist claimants in collecting benefits."

Some employees have taken their cases to the courts. Stanley Flowers, a fifty-eight-year-old truck driver of Richfield, Ohio, has filed suit against the Teamsters' Central States, Southeast and Southwest Area Pension Fund, which he says has denied him a pension on the basis of faulty record-keeping. Mr. Flowers applied for benefits in January 1971. His records showed he had thirty years of service under the pension plan, which would make him eligible for a $300-a-month benefit under the plan's early retirement provision. In August 1971, Teamster Local 407 of Cleveland, Ohio, denied his application, claiming that Flowers was short two years of qualifying. Flowers' suit charges that the union "has carried out a willful and malicious plan to deprive persons entitled to their pensions . . . by refusing to pay and continuing to request information of the applicant until he either dies or gives up attempting to collect." He is asking for $6000 in back payments and 1 million dollars as "punishment" to prevent the union from continuing the alleged practices.

Other employees have gone to court charging arbitrary action on the part of administrators or trustees in setting rules that denied them pensions. A number of cases have been brought by mine workers who have been denied benefits after a lifetime in the mines, sometimes because of new rules promulgated *after* they had met the old requirements. One mine worker retired in 1950 after meeting all the qualifications for a pension. He was fifty-six and would have been eligible to start receiving his benefits when he was sixty. One year before he was sixty, the United Mine Workers' Welfare and Retirement Fund adopted new rules, including the rule that miners would have to be working for an employer contributing to the plan when they retired. Under these requirements, this worker, along with hundreds of others, was not eligible for a pension. The court, however, upheld the right of the trustees to promulgate new rules so long as they did not take upon themselves "abusive and despotic powers which tend to prostitute the spirit of the fund." [9]

In another case, a pressman in New Hampshire qualified for a pension after working twenty years in the industry and reaching age sixty. He chose to continue working for a few more years. When he was sixty-three and applied for a pension, he was turned down. By that time, the rules had been changed to require twenty-five years in the industry and attainment of age sixty-five. He sued, urging that a retroactive amendment should not deprive him of benefit rights he could have obtained earlier. But the court upheld the right of the trustees to deny him a pension under the new rule.[10]

Recently, the courts have granted pensions in several cases involving mine workers who were denied pensions under rules set after they qualified.[11] However, the courts did not rule on the fairness of the regulations themselves but declared that it was the duty of the trustees to notify affected workers of the new rule, which they had not done. It is a very slight gain for pension plan participants that they must be notified of new rules when they are passed. There is still no legal basis for challenging the rules *per se*.[12]

Whether or not you receive a pension, then, is still determined by the way your plan trustees have sliced the pie. In some cases, you can avoid disappointment by finding out exactly what you have to do to qualify.

You should know the answers to these questions:
1. How many years of continuous service must you have to be eligible for a pension?

2. What constitutes a break in service (six months, two years, etc.), and must you be available for recall if laid off in order to retain your eligibility?
3. How are service credits counted? Does your plan require a certain number of hours per week or weeks per year, for example?
4. How old must you be to qualify?
5. Must you be employed by the company, or by a company that contributes to a multiemployer plan, at the time of retirement or for a certain period immediately before retirement?
6. Must you be a member of the union or union local when you retire to receive a pension?

These are the kinds of questions that should be answered clearly and simply by your company personnel manager or your union officials. Often they will merely give you a copy of the plan, which they are required to do by law. But the technical way in which most plans are written prevents many employees from understanding all the conditions. The U.S. Department of Labor is currently revising its requirements for communication of plan provisions to employees. (See Chapter XII.) But don't wait for your employer or union to explain your plan in simple terms. Ask them questions today; you have a right to know.

You may also want to do the following:
1. Ask how many employees are expected to receive benefits if they enter the plan at age twenty-five, thirty-five, forty, and so on. This will give you an idea of your chances for a benefit.
2. In order to avoid discrepancies later, ask for a personal accounting of your own pension credits to date. Ask for these reports periodically.
3. Before you retire, find out how to apply for a pension.

4. If you leave the company and have vested rights, be sure you know and follow the procedures for applying for benefits.
5. If you do qualify for a pension, make sure you know any conditions for retirees. Can you take another job in the industry? Is there a limit on your earnings in retirement?

VI

Playing Against the Economy

Peter Jalmer of Woodlynn, New Jersey, worked for the Baldwin-Lima-Hamilton Company in Eddystone, Pennsylvania, for thirty years. Now his plant has closed. Along with his job, Mr. Jalmer lost his chance to qualify for a pension. "I am too old to get another job, too young to collect social security," he says. His problem is rooted in the American economy and its constant fluctuations completely beyond his control.

The Baldwin-Lima-Hamilton Company operated for more than 100 years. It was at one time the world leader in the production of steam locomotives and at one point employed more than 20,000 workers. But the economy bypassed the company. "By the time Baldwin acknowledged the primacy of diesel-powered locomotives over the coal-burning steamers," said one newspaper account, "other enterprising firms had most of the market. Baldwin turned out its last locomotives, a pair of diesels, in 1956, and turned to heavy equipment manufacture, again lagging behind the competition."

As Baldwin-Lima-Hamilton struggled to keep up with a fast-moving economy, the company became involved in equally swift shifts in business organization. In 1965, the company was acquired by Armour & Company, a Chicago-based meat-packing plant. Armour, in turn, was acquired in 1970 by the Greyhound Corporation. Greyhound immediately began pressing to sever Baldwin-Lima-Hamilton from its conglomerate structure. The decision to close down the Eddystone plant was announced, with a loss of 1200 jobs.

These 1200 workers were caught up in common business changes that affect not one but millions of workers who find that the economy can deny them their pensions.

Look at your own situation. What will happen to your pension if your company relocates, closes down, or goes bankrupt? If you already have nonforfeitable benefit rights and if the pension fund has enough money, you may keep your pension. But usually this will happen only if you are older and have many years of service with the company. If you are under sixty years of age, you have reason to worry. One fifty-two year old worker had not yet met his pension plan's requirements when the company closed down. He lost his pension. His new job has pension coverage but "it does me no good," he wrote. He will have to retire at age sixty-five—two years before he can meet the fifteen-year service requirement under the new plan.

Another displaced employee wrote: "I worked for several years with a company and hoped to retire, but it was sold to another team. We got no restitution for our earned pensions, and the new team did not want to hire me back. I am fifty-seven—too old to get a job and too young to retire."

What do you do if your pension plan requires "continuous service" with companies under the union-bargained plan but the only jobs in your area are with nonunion firms? One man under such a plan worked for union companies for forty-eight years—except for *one year* when the only job he could find was nonunion. Later he was told that this one year constituted a "break in continuous service," and he was denied a pension. His alternative would have been to stay out of work for a year, something few people can afford to do.

All of these conditions affect thousands of workers each year. Job changes are a fact of life in the American economy. Business fluctuations cause layoffs, plant shutdowns, mergers, sale of companies, and bankruptcies. These in turn mean job changes or job losses for millions of workers. And because pensions are almost always tied to long, continuous service in one job or one industry, these economic shifts mean loss of pensions.

How many people work continuously for the same employer for twenty years, or even ten years? No one knows exactly. But what we do know is not reassuring. The *Monthly Labor Review* reported in 1968 that according to Social Security data, half of all men aged sixty to sixty-four had less than 15.1 years of continuous service with the same employer. For women in the same age bracket, half had less than 9.4 years of continuous service with the same employer.[1]

We also know that the American labor force is a mobile one. One study of job changes in the late fifties found approximately two million job changes each month![2] There is no reason to believe that this situation has changed significantly.

John Brock, fifty-six, a carpenter from Santa Cruz, California, was a member of the union local in Santa Barbara from 1946 until 1960 when he was hurt on a union job and dropped from membership for two years because he could not pay his dues. Later he rejoined the union but in 1964, unable to find work near his home, he moved to St. Louis to work for a year.

Later he went to Florida to work and then moved back to California. "I wrote to Los Angeles requesting my status on the pension plan and how long I would have to go to retire. I was immediately notified that I had lost all pension rights and monies contributed to my account . . . as I had incurred a break in my account due to my absence from California."

Mr. Brock's career is not unusual. Workers have to go where the jobs are. The trouble is, their pensions usually do not go with them.

Business and economic changes that can affect your pension drastically include layoffs, plant shutdowns, and company mergers.

Layoffs due to changes in the industry

Pensions are most common in the manufacturing sector where industries are subject to cutbacks in employment at short enough intervals to damage pension rights even where "liberal" vesting provisions are offered. Although all industries are subject to employment cutbacks, the giant defense industry is a chief example of how current vesting conditions fail to reflect the realities of the job scene.

Arthur L. McNealus, fifty-three, an electronics engineer, worked for defense contractors for twenty-three years. Despite "liberal" vesting provisions that grant benefit rights after ten years of service, he was not able to qualify for a pension under any of his employers' plans. He worked for six years for Grumman Aerospace where he was laid off during the phase-out of the Apollo contract. He also worked for Space Technology Laboratories (TRW), Fairchild-Stratos Corporation, Ford Instrument Company, FXR, and, most recently, United Aircraft Corporation, Norden Division, where he was laid off after fifteen months because of a cutback in the F-111 contract.

Although the defense industry pension plans are among the most "liberal" in the country—most have full vesting after ten or fifteen years of service—only a small percentage of employees are gaining benefits under these plans. One study found that 80 percent of the employees in the aerospace industry had less than the ten years of service required for vesting.[3]

Business shutdowns

The high rate of business failures and permanent cutbacks is another important factor causing loss of pension benefits. From 1954 through 1967, the annual number of business failures varied from 11,000 to 17,000.[4] The great majority of these firms—consistently more than 75 percent—expired before they had existed for ten years. For employees of firms where pension plans were offered, even "liberal" ten-year vesting would have done little good.[5]

Most of the businesses that shut down or cut back each year are fairly small, but not all are. A study of mass permanent layoffs between 1963 and 1965 found that some 525 firms separated 187,000 employees on permanent layoff basis. More than half (295) of the layoffs affected employees of all ages.[6]

Every day newspapers report business closings, relocations, or other changes, many involving employees of old, established firms. What happens to workers who lose their jobs in this way? A study by the U.S. Arms Control and Disarmament Agency looked at the effect of layoffs on employees of the giant Republic Aviation Company plant on Long Island, New York. In 1962 the plant was all but shut down with layoffs of more than 13,000 people because of a cutback in production of the F-105 bomber. Those laid off were concentrated in the 36 to 55 age group. More than half had fewer than ten years' service with Republic, so they did not qualify for the company's pension plan. The new jobs they found paid less well than their jobs at Republic and tended not to carry pension benefits. A higher percentage of those aged forty-five and over were in temporary jobs with no pension coverage.

The same pattern was seen when the Detroit-Packard plant shut down in mid-1956, laying off hundreds of workers. Most of the employees were forty or older. By the end of 1959, three years after the plant shut down, some 22 percent of the workers had failed to find new jobs, and another 20 percent had gotten service jobs, where pension coverage is sparse. The remaining 58 percent found jobs in manufacturing, but a high percentage (more than half of those over fifty) lost those jobs later, along with any pension coverage they might have had.[7]

Mergers and transfers

Reportedly more than 125,000 firms change hands every six months.[8] Although most of the firms are small, the number of employees involved is significant. Mergers and transfers may involve the closing of a plant or unit and substantial separation of employees with an accompanying loss of pension credits. In many cases the company or unit remains in operation but the pension plan is terminated by the new owner or merged with another pension plan.

The recent trend in conglomerate take-overs has particularly affected white-collar workers, who are more likely to lose their jobs when new management enters. Often conglomerates buy a new firm without ever intending to keep it going (it may be a tax write-off), and many employees at all levels lose their jobs.

A 1962 amendment to the Internal Revenue Code requires that when a pension plan is terminated, the employer must pay all the claims on the fund as long as the money lasts.* However, employees who are laid off *prior* to actual plan termination have no claim on the pension fund unless their credits have vested. Actual termination of the plan can be delayed by the employer until the work force has been drastically reduced and few employees remain with claims on the fund. In this way, employers can capture the use of substantial amounts of the money already contributed to their plans, while many or most former employees go empty-handed.

For example, in 1954 Packard merged with Studebaker to form the Studebaker-Packard Corporation. At that time, Packard employed about 10,250 employees. Packard began closing out almost immediately, but it was not until late 1958 that the company announced termination of the pension plan. By that time, employment in the plant was reduced to 625 employees.[9]

In April 1959 International Harvester Company announced the closing of its McCormack works in Chicago, giving 1962 as the date for closing. At the time, 3800 workers were employed in the plant. Between April 17, 1959, and March 1, 1961, 3000 workers were separated, of whom approximately 400 retired with pensions and 550 were terminated with eligibility for pensions at retirement age. Some 2000 employees lost their jobs without any benefits at all. Only 800 employees, who were still active or on layoff status in 1962, had claims on the fund when the plan terminated.

Any large-scale layoff, plant shutdown, or sale or merger, with accompanying loss of jobs, can result in making available large amounts of pension funds for the employer's use, *whether or not* the plan is formally terminated. Funds may be returned

---

* Section 401 (a) provides that "upon its termination or upon complete discontinuance of contributions under the plan, the rights of all employees to benefits accrued to the date of such discontinuance to the extent then funded, or the amounts credited to the employees' accounts, are nonforfeitable."

to the employer as "actuarial gains." This means that more employees leave the plan than was predicted when the plan was set up, leaving money on which no active employees have a claim. That money may then be used to pay the employer's contribution for current workers without his having to put in new money.

When Griggs, Cooper & Company, a wholesale grocery business in St. Paul, Minnesota, sold out to Consolidated Food Corporation in 1953, Consolidated continued the Griggs plan for the next two years but began a phase-out that separated 500 of the 580 employees, 85 percent of them without pension benefits. Finally, only seventy-five of Griggs' former employees were still employed by Consolidated and only forty-two of them were participants in the pension plan. Since so few of the separated employees received benefits, Consolidated had enough money already in the fund to relieve the company of making contributions for the remaining participants. During two full years of the plan, Consolidated obtained about $170,000 in pension premium credits as a result of the cancellation of the separated employees' annuity credits. Although the case was taken to court, the court refused to declare the plan terminated at the time of the wholesale layoffs, which would have given the separated employees a right to the paid-up benefits.[10]

Another example of the recapture of pension funds for the use of the employer was reported in *Harper's* magazine (December 1969) by Otto Friedrich, former editor of the *Saturday Evening Post*. When the *Post* was sold to a new owner many employees under the former ownership lost their jobs, but the pension plan was not terminated right away. At the time of the sale the magazine was in serious financial difficulties. Then, Friedrich reported, the new owner informed the remaining staff that he had "found" ten million dollars. According to Friedrich, "It turned out later that staff cuts had left a large surplus in the company's pension fund."

The way in which conglomerates have used pension funds was discussed at length during the 1970 House hearings on pension legislation. Representative John Dent, chairman of the subcommittee that held the hearings, concluded: "There have been increasing instances where a conglomerate takes over a going concern and completely severs all employees from the payroll. Then they pick up those that have reached their vested rights, set aside enough money in reserve to meet the requirements for paying a vested interest of the employees who had reached that vested right, and take all the rest of the money in the pension fund as a surplus, actuarial surplus. . . ."

The regulations of the Internal Revenue Service do contain provisions for determining whether "partial termination" occurs when large numbers of employees are excluded from the pension plan because of discharge, or because of amendments to the plan. The I.R.S. regulations do not set out guidelines for partial terminations but say merely that such cases will be determined by the "facts and circumstances." Up to now, these regulations have been ineffective in helping employees who are involved in layoffs prior to plan termination. A major reason is that the courts have refused to rule, or to uphold I.R.S. rulings, that plans must terminate along with massive employee separations. The precedent for court action was set in the suit brought by employees of the Consolidated Food Corporation who were separated without benefits prior to termination of their pension plan.[11] Their petition for benefit rights was upheld by the trial court, but that decision was reversed on appeal by the Minnesota Supreme Court. A number of similar actions have also been dismissed by the courts.

However, increasing recognition of the problem of layoffs

prior to plan terminations has led the I.R.S. to look more closely at plan terminations. For the first time, as of January 1972, the I.R.S. termination forms ask whether the total number of plan participants at termination is less than 20 percent of the previous year's total participants. The forms also ask whether the company has closed a plant or division during the year. It remains to be seen whether the information gained through these forms will lead to stricter enforcement of I.R.S. "partial termination" regulations. It is still advisable for employees involved in large-scale layoffs to write to the I.R.S. requesting a termination ruling. Although few, if any, employees have received substantial help from the agency in the past, increasing evidence of benefit loss in these situations could lead to a stricter regulatory approach. If the I.R.S. does not take action, or if it rules that the plan need not terminate along with the layoffs, employees may go to court to challenge that ruling.

In all of these business and economic shifts, the old doctrine that workers should be rewarded if they stay with one employer during most or all of their careers and penalized by loss of pension credits if they do not is clearly obsolete. A job change often has nothing to do with the employee's wishes. The "stable" middle-aged and older worker can be as easily affected by a change as the younger worker, with the difference that older workers suffer more by it. Too often they have not acquired vested pension rights under the old employer and cannot find new jobs or pension plans that will allow them to build up credits before they retire.

The pressing need now is to provide vesting requirements that will make it easier for workers to gain some benefit rights at an early age in order to protect themselves against job changes dictated by forces beyond their control. If you are a member of a union, you should find out whether your union officials support earlier vesting provisions, either in the contract bargaining process or through Federal legislation to establish minimum vesting standards for private pension plans, or both. (See Chapter X for proposed vesting legislation.) Some unions, notably the United Auto Workers Union and the United Steelworkers, have pressed hard for early vesting standards through bargaining and legislation. But few other unions are vocal in supporting vesting standards.

The major argument used by employers against earlier vesting is that it costs too much. Union leaders have traditionally preferred larger benefits at the expense of earlier vesting. Many unions and employers warn workers that their benefits will be reduced if they are given earlier vesting rights, but they fail to add that many employees will also lose *all* benefits, no matter how large, without earlier vesting.

The majority of employees who replied to our question (252 out of 352) said they favored earlier vesting provisions *even if benefits had to be reduced.* One union member from San Diego, California, wrote that he "would estimate that 90 percent of the employees would like to have more money deducted each week to add to retirement, even double it, with the understanding that after ten or fifteen years they would have a vested interest in the employer contribution, as well as the return of paycheck-deducted monies."

Some unions are dealing with the problem of workers' loss of credits toward a pension in ways other than earlier vesting. For example, some have entered into reciprocity agreements with other union-operated pension funds, thus allowing workers to transfer to jobs under these plans and take their pension credits with them. Reportedly, of the approximately 1300 negotiated multiemployer plans, covering about five million workers, reciprocity agreements now cover about half the workers enrolled in such funds.[12] A few unions have established national industry-wide plans allowing workers to move to different parts of the country without losing their pension credits. These unions include the United Mine Workers, Amalgamated Clothing Workers of America, International Ladies' Garment Workers, and International Brotherhood of Electrical Workers.[13] Agreements like these mean that pensions become "portable," at least within the limited range of jobs and unions covered by the reciprocity agreements.

One pension plan, the Teachers Insurance and Annuity Association (TIAA), covering college and university employees, has for a number of years contained provisions that protect the members' pensions almost entirely. All contributions under the plan vest *immediately,* without age and service requirements. Members of the plan can transfer freely from any of the covered institutions (600 cooperating colleges, universities, independent schools, and similar institutions) to another and maintain participation in the plan. If a member becomes employed at an institution that is not covered under TIAA, he can continue contributions on his own if he wishes.

Senators Harrison Williams and Jacob Javits have introduced legislation that would set up a system to provide "portable" pensions on a voluntary basis. Employers and unions could voluntarily transfer to a fund, administered by the Secretary of Labor, money credited to an individual's pension account when that individual leaves the plan. These funds would either be held for the employee until his retirement or paid over to the new pension plan in which he was participating.

VII

Winner Take Nothing

Joseph Wojnarowski was sixty-four when he found that he would receive no benefit from his pension fund after forty-two years with the Haws Refractories of Johnstown, Pennsylvania. He had not been laid off, nor had the company shut down. The problem was that the pension fund itself had run out of money.

Because of a decline in business, the company had reduced its contributions to the pension plan until, finally, the plan no longer had enough money to pay all the claims. Wojnarowski was a union official, but he had no idea how his pension plan was being funded or whether contributions had been reduced or were being made at all. He had never seen any data regarding the soundness of the fund. Later he and co-worker John Gojmerac testified before a congressional committee. "We should have been notified that the thing was going down like it was" Gojmerac said, "and not just drop a bomb out of the sky and say there was nothing there." [1]

Dick Barnes reported in an Associated Press series the similar troubles of a small union pension plan, the Hat Trimmers Union Local 7 Retirement Fund.[2] In 1968 the fund paid out $9945 to its thirty-nine retired pensioners but had income of only $5945. To decrease the deficit, the employers' contributions were increased by 6 percent. However, the deficit continued and the benefit payments were reduced from $25 a month to $20 a month. When the deficit for 1969 became even worse, the union wrote its members in the summer of 1969: "Under the circumstances, the trustees have resolved to suspend all pension payments for a period of one year after making the enclosed payment covering the months of July, August and September, 1969. The next payment will be made on October 1st, 1970." At that time, the union had only twenty-six active members on whose behalf employer contributions were being made. Under the terms of the plan, the employers were obligated only to make certain contributions that were based on a percentage of their payroll. They had no obligation to provide certain benefits to retirees. The hatmakers' business was falling off, indicating that future contributions would be still lower. As a result, the New York State Insurance Department finally obtained a court order for the fund's liquidation. Both the retired workers who counted on their monthly benefits and the active workers who expected them were helpless. After the meager amount left in the fund was paid out, they were left with nothing.

Statistics indicate that one in every fourteen plans qualified by the Internal Revenue Service terminates. In 1971 alone, some 3335 plans folded, affecting more than 125,000 workers.*

---

* An eleven-year study by the Bureau of Labor Statistics (B.L.S.) reported an average of 500 plans terminating each year and affecting some 25,000 employees a year, or

Regulations of the Internal Revenue Service require that when a plan is terminated the employer must pay out all the money in the fund. The catch is that most pension funds don't have enough money to pay all their liabilities. A lot of people lose and there is nothing they can do about it.

The United Auto Workers Union recently studied the termination of UAW-negotiated pension plans over a ten-year period from 1959 through 1968.[4] In those ten years, ninety-nine UAW pension plans terminated. Almost three-fourths of the workers covered by those plans (73.4 percent) received either no benefits at all or reduced benefits because the plans did not have enough money.*

The workers who suffered the most from these terminations were those between the ages of forty and sixty.[5] Workers above the age of sixty were usually paid their full benefits, and workers below the age of forty had at least a reasonable chance of getting pensions on other jobs, but workers in the forty to sixty

---

about one-tenth of 1 percent of all workers under private pension plans.[3] The B.L.S. concluded that terminations have not adversely affected pension rights to a "substantial degree." However, Merton C. Bernstein and others have pointed out that the number reported in the B.L.S. study probably represents no more than a fraction of the total number of employees who are actually affected by plan terminations. The study was limited to plan participants at the time of termination, while many employees, sometimes most employees, are laid off prior to termination, during production cutbacks and other employment changes that usually go along with plan terminations. (See testimony by Professor Bernstein before the Senate Special Committee on Aging, February 18, 1970.)

A more recent study by Charles D. Spencer and Associates, Inc., based on statistics released by the Internal Revenue Service, shows an increased number of terminations; a total of 19,989 plans terminated to the end of 1971 from the time the I.R.S. first started to qualify plans. In some instances, employees are brought under a new plan, such as a plan operated by an acquiring company, after their old plan is terminated. See "Employee Benefit Plan Review—Research Reports," looseleaf pension plan service published by Charles D. Spencer and Associates, Inc., 222 West Adams Street, Chicago, Illinois 60606.

* Of the covered workers, 73.4 percent received either no benefits or less than full benefits; approximately 39 percent received no benefits at all; only 26.6 percent of the total received full benefits, mostly those who were already retired or eligible to retire.

age bracket had many years of service for which they were paid little or nothing in pension benefits, and they had considerably less chance than younger people of new jobs with pension coverage. More than half of the UAW plans (52.6 percent) paid no benefits to workers under age fifty when they terminated, and more than one-quarter of the plans (26.3 percent) paid no benefits to those between fifty and sixty.

Some plans have so little money when they terminate that even retirees have their benefits reduced. For example, when the Packard pension plan terminated in 1958 (after Packard merged with Studebaker to form the Studebaker-Packard Corporation), the company announced it would reduce benefits to retirees by 65 percent because there was not enough money in the fund. At that time, 1930 retirees with average company service of twenty-six years were receiving pensions that averaged $59 a month. Eventually, a settlement was reached whereby the company agreed to provide retirees with 85 percent of their full benefits, reducing the average payment to $50 a month.[6]

The potential loss of benefits through plan terminations is large indeed since the majority of pension plans do not have enough money on hand to cover all benefit claims for years after they have been established. The Senate Labor Subcommittee has reported the kinds of deficiencies that exist today in the pension plans of large reputable companies. The Western Union Telegraph Company, as of July 30, 1969, had assets in its fund that amounted to only 12 percent of its liabilities. In other words, if the Western Union plan were terminated on that date, only 12 percent of all benefit claims could be paid. Uniroyal, Inc., was underfunded to the extent that its assets amounted to less than 35 percent of its liabilities for the same year. The New York Hotel Trades Council Pension Fund had assets comprising only slightly over one-fourth of their vested liabilities in 1969.[7] In each case, officials for the companies said they were simply following routine procedures for funding—procedures that are considered acceptable under any regulations existing today.

You must remember, too, that "liabilities" include only those benefit credits that have vested. They do not include the years of service of employees who have not yet acquired vested rights.

Proposals for public reinsurance of pension plans to insure payment of vested benefit claims when plans do not have sufficient monies in the fund have been pending before Congress for several years. The United Auto Workers Union and the United Steelworkers have been vocal in support of reinsurance. UAW President Leonard Woodcock has argued for "public reinsurance of private pension funds—similar to the insurance provided since the 1930's for bank deposits, and akin to the backstop federal protection the President asks [and has gotten] for investors." [8]

Other unions, notably members of the AFL-CIO, are not supporting reinsurance because their industries are comprised mainly of smaller, low-wage companies, and they fear that higher costs would force these employers to reduce pension coverage or benefits.

Employers argue against Federal insurance, claiming that most private pension plans are soundly funded, that few people have lost benefits as the result of plan terminations, and that it would not be fair for employers with fully funded plans to support the expense of insuring plans that are not.

Employees, however, think differently. Of those responding to our questionnaire, 490 said yes, they thought pension funds should be insured so that if there is not enough money in the fund the promised benefits can be paid; only twelve said no. Further, 338 of the respondents favored pension insurance even if employee benefits had to be reduced to cover the added costs; 101 did not.

Reinsurance could protect you not only if your plan terminates without sufficient funds, but also if your fund becomes insolvent for any reason: if the monies in the fund have been ill-managed or abused (See Chapter VIII); if your employer cuts contributions below the prescribed rate or discontinues them altogether because of business declines; if the prescribed rates of contribution are not high enough to cover the costs of the liabilities.

Insuring pension plans against such possibilities is not enough: employers should be required to assume greater responsibility for meeting the benefits promised under the plan. The most important proposed means of increasing the employer's responsibility is setting minimum Federal funding standards.

The United Steelworkers, among other unions, has called for Federal legislation to require a certain level of funding in all plans that seek tax-exempt status. I. W. Abel, president of the United Steelworkers, has said that the present situation, which gives the employer complete discretion in financing the plan, leaves the door open for companies to not fund or deliberately to underfund their plans.[9] It also allows an irresponsible owner who intends to go out of business after a few years to contribute only minuscule amounts, far from enough to pay a significant part of the claims.

Others have suggested that companies should be legally liable for meeting vested benefit rights.[10] Pension rights would then be legally enforcible against the general assets (as opposed to just the pension plan assets) of the employer in the event a plan terminates with insufficient monies to cover all claims. Such responsibility might encourage employers to fund vested benefits in full.

It should be noted that these proposals would insure coverage only of *vested* benefit rights. The ultimate goal should be the coverage of all service credits, whether vested or not.

Most employers and some unions oppose regulations that would set minimum funding standards or impose greater responsibility on employers for meeting benefit claims. Employers argue that they need flexibility in funding in order to allow for fluctuations in business from year to year. Multiemployer unions, particularly those in the apparel industries, oppose funding standards for fear that minimum funding would reduce the number of companies offering plans since these firms tend to be small, low-profit firms.[11] Many union officials favor higher benefits, which are made possible by underfunding pension plans. If pension funds had to have a certain level of monies on hand at any one time, they might have to reduce the size of the benefits currently being paid out.

As long as employers are not held responsible for putting enough money in the pension fund to cover all or most of the claims, employees bear a large burden of risk, and unfortunately most employees don't even know it. There is no way for them to enforce their benefit rights when a plan terminates without sufficient funds or for any other reason cannot pay them the pensions they expect. Most employees are dependent on the continued solvency of their company and on the employer's willingness—virtually unenforced—to make sufficient contributions to cover their future pensions. There is little you can do to protect your pension until there are stricter funding regulations and/or provisions for plan insurance. You can, however, avoid Gojmerac's "bomb out of the sky" by knowing the answers to the following:

1. Is there a separate fund for pension contributions or are benefits paid from your employer's operating budget? (The latter is a very high-risk plan.)

2. If there is a separate fund, to what extent do your employer's contributions cover both benefit credits as they are earned and "past service credits"?
3. Does the employer make contributions according to a fixed actuarial schedule? Has he discontinued or reduced his scheduled contributions at any time?
4. If the plan were to terminate today, what percentage of your plan's liabilities (existing benefit claims of both retired and active workers) could be paid out of assets (funds now on hand)?
5. If the plan were to terminate today without sufficient funds to cover all claims, how would the money be distributed? (For example, if you are between the ages of forty and fifty, or fifty and sixty, and have vested rights, would you get anything? Or would your benefits be reduced and by how much?)
6. At what date will the plan be "fully funded," that is, able to pay all *vested* benefits?

If you find that your employer is not making regular contributions or has reduced them, or if a large amount of liabilities is not covered, you should go immediately to your union or your employer and ask for an accounting. You may find that your pension is not as secure as you believe.

VIII

The Dealers

Much of the money needed to give benefits to more people would be right there in the pension funds themselves if those funds were always handled wisely. Your interest in a well-managed fund is obvious. The size of your benefit, as well as its security, depends not only on initial contributions to the fund but also on the way it is managed. If the money is squandered, or used for the self-interest of the employer or the union, or unwisely invested, you and the other beneficiaries pay the price.

Although most pension fund money goes into trust funds that are theoretically beyond the control of employers and unions, in reality this money is subject to manipulation, primarily because employers and unions can govern the ways these funds are invested. Plan participants are not informed of and have no control over the investment of their funds. It is shocking how few government regulations there are to cover the management of the 152.8 billion dollars in private pension funds. Information that must be filed with the U.S. Department of Labor under the Welfare and Pension Plans Disclosure Act consists chiefly of a copy of the plan and an annual report containing very limited details about the way the plan is administered. Even where there are laws against embezzlement and other abuses, illegal actions don't necessarily come to the attention of officials. The government has taken action only in the most flagrant cases of fund abuse, and these have come to the attention of Federal authorities generally by accident, not through routine reporting and investigation.

A striking example is what happened to the pension monies of the 60,000 members of the Journeymen Barbers, Hairdressers, Cosmetologists and Proprietor's International Union. In 1966, the barbers' pension fund had assets totaling $21,000,000, managed by the Indiana National Bank. Then a man named Thomas A. Shaheen appeared, offering his services as investment consultant. According to Edgar Sanders, the union's secretary-treasurer, Shaheen "came in to talk to the pension committee. He criticized the bank's investment decisions. He was trying to say they had made only so much money, that he could have made more. He convinced the board the bank was losing the fund money." [1]

The pension committee apparently was pleased when Shaheen told them his services would cost them nothing—that certain interests wanting to borrow money from the pension fund would pay his fees! Committee members apparently did not take the trouble to investigate Shaheen's qualifications to handle the fund. If they had, they would have found that several months before he approached them, Shaheen had filed for personal bankruptcy in Chicago.

After Shaheen became consultant to the fund, the fund sold

60 percent of its common stock holdings and made $11,000,000 worth of mortgage loans. Among others, the fund made a loan of $500,000 to the Winthrop Lawrence Corporation, of which Shaheen was the chief executive. The corporation's board chairman was Lamont duPont Copeland, Jr., son of the board chairman of E. I. duPont de Nemours & Company of Delaware. In 1970 Copeland filed for bankruptcy listing debts of some $60,000,000 and assets of less than half that amount.

Shaheen told the barbers at a union convention in May 1968 that the loans were guaranteed against loss by bonds issued by insurers. At the head of the insurers was the Prudence Mutual Casualty Company of Chicago. About the time loan delinquencies began to show up in the fund, Prudence Mutual was revealed to have insufficient assets and soon went into receivership.

The barbers' fund was headed on the same route. In July 1971 it too went into court-appointed receivership following the indictment on thirty-six counts of Shaheen, one of his associates, Max Block, Jr., of New York, and Joseph de Paola, union president and pension fund board chairman. Among other things, they were charged with making questionable loans, and in the case of de Paola, with taking $29,000 in illegal fees, kickbacks, and commissions.

De Paola pleaded guilty on one count and was sentenced to a year in jail. Block was tried and acquitted. Shaheen is a fugitive, believed to be out of the country, and has yet to come to trial.[2]

As of July 1971 the fund had invested in forty-four loans with an aggregate unpaid balance of $11,799,918. Its assets, which had once totaled $21,000,000, had declined to $13,490,964.[3]

The fund's financial troubles had showed up long before the court indictments. On October 13, 1969, an accounting firm concluded that the plan would be able to pay its promised benefits only if the fund earned 11 percent on its investments after expenses each year and increased its size by 1500 members a year. By the end of 1970 membership units in the fund showed a decline of 10,000 members over the past four years. Projected investment income that year was only 7.3 percent.[4]

But although the fund's difficulties were known to the accountants and the fund officials involved, the participants themselves were in the dark. So were government regulators who, had they known about it, might have attempted to stop the wheeling and dealing with union members' money. The illegalities came to light only by chance after the Barbers' Fund offered a deal involving the guarantee of a questionable loan to a Los Angeles, California, bank. A bank officer concluded that anyone offering such a deal did not have the best interests of the fund participants first and foremost on his mind. He went to the U.S. Labor Department with information that led to exposure of the erstwhile investment consultant.[5] It was an investigation that might never have occurred. Had it not been for the vigilant bank officer, the alleged kickback arrangement between the so-called consultant, the borrowers who paid him, and the fund board chairman could conceivably have continued until the fund was bankrupt.

Another case of abuse of pension plans uncovered recently involved the Teamsters' Union Central States, Southeast and Southwest Area Pension Fund. This fund is one of the country's largest pension plans, with reportedly more than half a billion dollars in assets. Two-thirds of the money is in mortgages.[6]

Costly abuses of Teamsters Central States Fund money were revealed by chance when informants gave information to

newspaper reporters and members of Congress. Follow-up investigations by teams of journalists and Justice Department investigators uncovered still more details of the Fund's mismanagement.

In this fashion it was discovered that a Detroit real estate company had received an increase on a loan from $1,050,000 to $2,500,000 by paying a kickback of $10,000 to a New York mortgage broker. This information came out in the trial of a former auditor of the fund who was convicted for a kickback arrangement on a deal involving a Teamsters Central States Fund loan. The auditor was brought to trial after a tip-off led government investigators to seek an indictment.

Information brought to light in this case pointed to a pattern of kickbacks in connection with the fund's loans and loan applications. Seven indictments were handed down in New York Federal courts in 1969 and 1970 naming twenty-five defendants, including reputed underworld figures. Six persons were convicted and one pleaded guilty in two trials.

The fund's dealings included a series of loans totaling some $53,000,000 to a lush California resort. The largest loan of $35,000,000 had a second mortgage for security. Additional loans went to Las Vegas hotels. The fund has also had a series of foreclosures on Nevada property. After foreclosing on one shopping center in Las Vegas, the fund purchased the center at auction for $1,500,000, sold it the same day, and financed the sale 100 percent by giving the new owners a $1,500,000 loan.

Amendments to the Welfare and Pension Plans Disclosure Act in 1962 made theft, embezzlement, bribery, and kickbacks Federal crimes. They also gave the Secretary of Labor limited investigatory authority and the right to issue regulations. Those amendments, however, have been a failure. In 1970 hearings before the House General Subcommittee on Labor, numerous cases of abuse and self-dealing were disclosed. At those hearings, then Secretary of Labor George P. Shultz testified that "the current picture is one of inadequate, weak and unrealistic safeguards and remedies. . . . The present disclosure requirements and the Labor Department's investigatory authority are so limited that virtually none of the known breaches of fiduciary responsibility were disclosed as a result of reports filed under the Welfare and Pension Plans Disclosure Act or through exercise of the Department's investigative authority under the law." [7]

Further, although persons convicted under the Act may be fined or sentenced to jail, workers whose monies have been wasted or lost are without legal remedy to recover those funds.

Bearing out Mr. Shultz' point, irregularities in another pension fund, the United Mine Workers' Welfare and Retirement Fund, were brought to light not by a government regulatory agency but by mine workers themselves. Millions of dollars of mine workers' pension monies were already beyond recovery when the abuse of the fund by the fund trustees was unfolded through a court suit. The case illustrates the way that fund trustees may use monies in pension funds, ostensibly set aside for beneficiaries, to further the interests of the union, the employer, or the trustees themselves.

In the case of *Blankenship et al. v. Boyle et al.* (Tony Boyle, UMW president), the U.S. District Court for the District of Columbia found the following abuses: first, the trustees had deposited as much as $75,000,000, or 44 percent of the fund's total resources, in the National Bank of Washington, where the money was drawing no interest whatsoever. The union held 74 percent of the stock of the bank and was able to use the retirement fund's money without paying one cent of interest. The court found that during that period the pension fund hearings before the House General Subcommittee on Labor, numerous cases of abuse and self-dealing were disclosed. At those hearings, then Secretary of Labor George P. Shultz testified that "the current picture is one of inadequate, weak and unrealistic safeguards and remedies. . . . The present disclosure requirements and the Labor Department's investigatory authority are so limited that virtually none of the known breaches of fiduciary responsibility were disclosed as a result of reports filed under the Welfare and Pension Plans Disclosure Act or through exercise of the Department's investigative authority under the law." [7]

Further, although persons convicted under the Act may be fined or sentenced to jail, workers whose monies have been wasted or lost are without legal remedy to recover those funds.

Bearing out Mr. Shultz' point, irregularities in another pension fund, the United Mine Workers' Welfare and Retirement Fund, were brought to light not by a government regulatory agency but by mine workers themselves. Millions of dollars of mine workers' pension monies were already beyond recovery when the abuse of the fund by the fund trustees was unfolded through a court suit. The case illustrates the way that fund trustees may use monies in pension funds, ostensibly set aside for beneficiaries, to further the interests of the union, the employer, or the trustees themselves.

In the case of *Blankenship et al. v. Boyle et al.* (Tony Boyle, UMW president), the U.S. District Court for the District of Columbia found the following abuses: first, the trustees had deposited as much as $75,000,000, or 44 percent of the fund's total resources, in the National Bank of Washington, where the money was drawing no interest whatsoever. The union held 74 percent of the stock of the bank and was able to use the retirement fund's money without paying one cent of interest. The court found that during that period the pension fund

THE DEALERS 69

newspaper reporters and members of Congress. Follow-up investigations by teams of journalists and Justice Department investigators uncovered still more details of the Fund's mismanagement.

In this fashion it was discovered that a Detroit real estate company had received an increase on a loan from $1,050,000 to $2,500,000 by paying a kickback of $10,000 to a New York mortgage broker. This information came out in the trial of a former auditor of the fund who was convicted for a kickback arrangement on a deal involving a Teamsters Central States Fund loan. The auditor was brought to trial after a tip-off led government investigators to seek an indictment.

Information brought to light in this case pointed to a pattern of kickbacks in connection with the fund's loans and loan applications. Seven indictments were handed down in New York Federal courts in 1969 and 1970 naming twenty-five defendants, including reputed underworld figures. Six persons were convicted and one pleaded guilty in two trials.

The fund's dealings included a series of loans totaling some $53,000,000 to a lush California resort. The largest loan of $35,000,000 had a second mortgage for security. Additional loans went to Las Vegas hotels. The fund has also had a series of foreclosures on Nevada property. After foreclosing on one shopping center in Las Vegas, the fund purchased the center at auction for $1,500,000, sold it the same day, and financed the sale 100 percent by giving the new owners a $1,500,000 loan.

Amendments to the Welfare and Pension Plans Disclosure Act in 1962 made theft, embezzlement, bribery, and kickbacks Federal crimes. They also gave the Secretary of Labor limited investigatory authority and the right to issue regulations. Those amendments, however, have been a failure. In 1970 lost some $12,000,000 in earnings. In other words, if the funds had been invested in interest-drawing stocks or bonds, the pension fund would have been increased by $12,000,000. In ordering the union and the union bank to pay $12,000,000 to the welfare and retirement fund, the court said that "the beneficiaries [of the pension fund] were not in any way assisted by these cash accumulations, while the union and bank profited."

Further, the court found that the trustees were using pension fund monies to advance the interests of the union rather than those of beneficiaries by purchasing large blocks of electric utility stocks. The trustees also loaned pension money to the Eaton Company, a coal company with close ties to the union, to buy electric utility stocks. The union and the Eaton Company then pressured the management of these utilities to buy only union-mined coal. The court found that these activities "present a clear case of self-dealing on the part of trustees Lewis and Schmidt and constituted a breach of trust."

The court also found that the UMW pension fund trustees had failed to collect the royalties owed to the fund by the West Kentucky Coal Company. The UMW Welfare and Retirement Fund is financed by collecting from coal operators participating in the pension fund a royalty of 80 cents per ton of coal. The West Kentucky Coal Company at one time owed as much as $700,000 in back royalties. The large coal company was controlled by the union, in conjunction with the Eaton Company, through the union's heavy stock interest in the company. The court said that the union representative acting as a retirement fund trustee should have disqualified himself from decisions involving royalty collections from that company.

Many transactions that result in the loss of money that belongs to fund beneficiaries are not even considered illegal. The result is that employers can freely and legally indulge in financial irregularities with pension funds that may be as harmful for plan participants as secret deals and kickbacks, which are subject to prosecution.

A frequent practice of pension funds that is not illegal is the investment of fund monies in securities owned by the employer company or in loans—often big loans—to the company itself. For example, the retirement plan of the Solo Cup Company of Chicago invested $890,000 of its less than $2,000,000 in cup-making machines, which it leased to the parent company. It loaned another $500,000 to the company so it could buy some more cup-making machines.[8]

The Whitaker Cable Company told a Senate committee that among the real estate holdings of the company's pension fund was the company's own office building, purchased by the pension trust for $465,000.[9]

The D.C. Transit Company testified that its pension plan made a secured loan of approximately $2,300,000 to the company in 1968. Company officials stated they saw no conflict of interest in the employer having such a large obligation to the pension fund since the promissory note was secured by the employer's real estate, the value of which was larger than the amount of the obligation. Yet the pension fund now has a deficit because it is owed $2,300,000 by the employer.[10]

The Genesco Company has said that approximately $15,000,000 of its $80,000,000 pension trust fund is invested in its own securities.[11]

The profit-sharing fund operated by Sears, Roebuck & Company invests over 80 percent of the nearly 3 billion dollars in the fund in Sears stock. This amounts to approximately 25 percent of all the outstanding stock.[12]

Approximately 28 percent of the Winn-Dixie Corporation profit-sharing fund's assets is invested in common stock or properties of Winn-Dixie Stores, Inc., or its subsidiaries. Some

$960,000 of these funds is invested in mortgage loans to corporations in which officers or directors of Winn-Dixie, Inc., have substantial interest. Some of them are owned outright by these persons. A return of 5.65 percent was earned on this investment to the fund.[13]

Because such potential conflicts of interest are allowed, plan beneficiaries suffer outright losses. For example, pension trustees of the McGrory Corporation, who were also officers of the corporation, purchased shares of McGrory stock for the fund at the same time that they were selling their own holdings. When the fund quit buying, the stock prices dropped by two-thirds. The fund lost $4,500,000 in these and other securities transactions.[14]

In another case, the Employee Savings and Profit Sharing Fund of the Kropp Forge Company of Chicago bought 206,318 shares of the company's stock from two company officers who were leaving the company for $3 a share. The stock was worth $1.875 a share at the time, according to a report the fund filed with the Labor Department.[15]

Whether or not abuses or losses occur, the practice of investing plan assets in securities insured by the funding employer is questionable. Even if such investments have a high expected rate of return compared with other securities, the practice ties the participants' retirement income to the fortunes of the same company on which they are dependent for their future wages.

Proposals are before Congress to limit to 10 percent the investments of a pension fund in the stock of the company operating the plan. Other proposals would attempt to enforce stricter fiduciary responsibility of fund trustees and require fuller disclosure of financial undertakings to the fund's participants and to the U.S. Departments of Labor and Treasury. (See Chapter XI for legislative proposals.)

74   YOU AND YOUR PENSION

In addition to misuse or questionable use of pension fund money by fund trustees, unions, and employers, there are still other threats to the size of your fund:

The managers of your fund can eat into your benefits by spending large sums to administer the fund. Sometimes this involves the acquisition of an expensive computer, or other equipment, which the fund does not need. Sometimes managers may be enriching themselves or their friends. In one instance, three of the five trustees administering the pension and profit-sharing plans of a corporation were past or present officers of the corporation. In one year, these five trustees received more than $300,000 in trustees' fees alone. In addition, the pension and profit-sharing plans paid more than $130,000 to a separate corporation controlled by these same trustees, which was established to administer and invest the funds.[16]

In another case, the Painters Pension Fund of Suffolk County, N.Y., paid $19,184 in insurance commissions to a man whose wife worked for the fund. He had little previous insurance experience.[17]

Expensive junkets to conferences of questionable benefit to fund beneficiaries may be paid for out of pension fund monies. The secretary-treasurer of the Hotel & Restaurant Employees and Bartenders International Union recently told union members that their pension fund was spending large amounts of money so that officials could attend the conferences of the National Foundation of Health, Welfare and Pension Plans, Inc. "The attendance at these conferences is expensive and frequently a waste of the monies of the trust, which money is really the property of our members," he wrote in the union magazine in October 1970. "There is not only an annual conference but there are other conferences during the year which are unnecessary and equally expensive. The sites and accommodations for these conferences are obviously not selected on a business basis but rather on the basis of recreation and vacation."

"Ordinarily," he continued, "where it would be sufficient that the trust fund plan administrator plus one or two trustees go, the attractiveness of the trip compels the entire board of trustees to attend. As a matter of fact, frequently officers of the union who are not even trustees attend the conferences at the local union's expense."

The union official was also angered, it is fair to add, by the fact that the Foundation had held its conferences in nonunion hotels or in hotels organized by another union. His point is nonetheless well taken, and you would do well to be wary about the fees and other fringe benefits your fund is giving to trustees.

What percentage of your fund is going for administration? The amount spent will, of course, depend on the size of the fund. Small funds will spend a larger percentage of their monies on administration than larger ones. But if your fund is spending 10 percent, or even as much as 5 percent, on administration, there is a good chance your money is being wasted.

Poor investments are another possible threat to your pension fund. Under most pension plans, the employer and/or union appoints a third-party trustee to undertake the investment management of the pension fund. Most are handled by banks and insurance companies, but independent investment firms also handle a sizeable number of pension accounts. The security of your pension under such plans depends to a large extent on the ability of these institutions to handle your money wisely.

As of December 1971, nearly one-third of all private pension assets, an estimated 45.4 billion dollars, were handled by insurance companies.[18] Most pension funds held by insurance companies go into company reserves whose investments are governed by fairly strict laws, including the provision that only 10 percent can be invested in common stock. Recently, insurance companies have been putting more pension monies into separate accounts that are not governed by these restrictive investment regulations. With investment leeway, insurance companies can promise to increase a fund's earnings and can become more competitive with banks in attracting pension funds.

An estimated 106.4 billion dollars of private pension assets were in noninsured funds at the end of 1971. Of these monies, bank trust departments managed about four-fifths.[19] A small but growing percentage of noninsured pension funds is handled by investment advisory firms that have been increasingly competitive in the battle for pension funds during the last decade.

Most noninsured pension funds—those held by banks and other financial institutions in separate trust funds—are invested in common stock and corporate bonds. In 1970, 53.3 percent of the assets of private noninsured pension funds was invested in common stock and 30.6 percent in corporate and other bonds.[20] The percentage of assets in common stock rose still higher in 1971. By the end of 1971, common stock in pension fund portfolios amounted to 84.8 billion dollars at market value and accounted for 68 percent of pension fund assets.[21]

A bank that handles a pension fund may have one or more co-trustees. But banks are sole trustees in four-fifths of all bank trusteed plans.[22] They have sole authority over three-fourths of their pension account stockholdings in making investment decisions; that is, they make purchases and sales of stock and vote stock proxies without consultation with anyone. (This is true for less than 30 percent of all personal trust and estate account shares and for less than 10 percent of shares in agency accounts other than pension plan accounts.)[23]

In theory, the trustee in charge of investing your pension funds is supposed to act solely in your best interest, that is, the interests of the plan beneficiaries. However, it is the employer or union, not the beneficiaries, who determines the investment objectives, and your employer's investment objectives may not serve your interests. He may want pension monies invested in his own company. He may instruct the trustees to invest in high-risk stock. The expected return on investments increases with the acceptance of greater risk, and many employers and unions, especially in industries where profits are low, tend to accept higher risks, and therefore future earnings of the plan may be less safe. But this is contrary to the interests of employees in a modest but secure level of benefits for their retirement as opposed to a more generous but highly uncertain level.[24]

A major problem with pension investment management is that participants in the pension-benefit plan are not considered to have legitimate interests as investors.[25] Thus, although your retirement security depends on the successful investment management of your pension fund, you are generally not informed of its operations, its investment policies, or changes in its management. And plan participants have no recourse if they are dissatisfied with the performance of the bank or other funding agent.

While investment goals that conflict with the interests of plan participants are one problem, even more disturbing is the *lack* of performance goals in any terms for many pension funds. Overall pension fund performance has been extraordinarily low. In 1971 noninsured funds earned an average of only 4 percent.[26] Recently, more employers and unions have attempted to improve their funds' investment performance by dividing the monies among banks, insurance companies, and independent investment firms, which compete with each other for the best returns. Some pension funds have begun hiring brokerage firms to evaluate the performance of each of these investment institutions. However, financial experts still marvel at the laxity with which most corporations oversee their pension funds. *Institutional Investor* reports that corporations that spend thousands of dollars and work-hours setting production goals for their own profits have never set specific, well-thought-out performance goals for their pension funds. According to one recent study of United States pension funds, 76 percent of the companies replying to a questionnaire said they did not plan to make their now vague performance goals more specific.[27]

There are few guidelines today against which to assess the performance of a pension portfolio in terms of the maximum possible earnings with the minimum acceptable risk. If assessments are made, beneficiaries have little if anything to say about them. For example, if your pension fund earned 12 percent but at a very high risk, are your interests adequately served? Would you prefer that the fund earned 6 percent at lower risk? How does your fund's performance compare with others? Are you assured that these kinds of assessments are being made by qualified financial experts? Or made at all?

Full disclosure of investments to plan participants would be a beginning toward greater assurance that banks and other funding agents act in accordance solely with your interests.

IX

The Payoff

What can you expect to get from your private pension if you do manage to qualify? Most people get less than $1000 a year, according to the latest figures. While this is better than getting no benefit at all, it is not much.

In 1967, the last year for which a breakdown of private pension benefits is available, half of the couples receiving private pensions got less than $970 a year, half the unmarried men received less than $865; and half the unmarried women received less than $665.[1]

Add this to the median Social Security payment for 1967 and you do not get very much. That year, half of the couples receiving OASDHI (Social Security) retirement benefits got less than $1555; half the unmarried men, $1080; and half the unmarried women, $860.[2]

More recently, the Senate Labor Subcommittee studied

benefits paid by 764 private pension plans covering 11.6 million workers and having assets of more than 30.7 billion dollars. Among all plans the median monthly benefit for normal retirement was $99 a month.[3] The study noted that even if the median private pension benefit of $99 a month is added to the median Social Security retirement payment of $129 a month, the total is only $228, *less* than what the government estimates is necessary to sustain an urban retired couple at a bare minimum. (The Bureau of Labor Statistics estimated in January 1970 that an income of $241 a month is required for an urban couple to maintain minimum sustenance.)[4]

The Senate Subcommittee also found that larger plans gave relatively larger benefits. For plans with less than 1000 participants, the median monthly payment for normal retirement was $96, and the median payments for early and disability retirement were less than $50. In contrast, the monthly medians paid by plans with 1000 or more participants were $121 for normal retirement, $99 for early retirement, and $79 for disability retirement.[5]

In 1970 the average outlay per private pension beneficiary was $1654.[6] It should be noted, however, that the *average* pension benefit does not reflect what *most* people get. In contrast to Social Security benefits, private pensions cover a broad range because they are based on length of continuous service and past earnings. Thus, a few people are getting comparatively large benefits while many others, with smaller wages and fewer years of credited service on which to earn benefits, get smaller pensions.[7]

Why are private pension benefits for most people so low? Some of the reasons were discussed in the previous chapter: money in pension funds may be siphoned off by unscrupulous administrators or mismanaged. But there are other factors that can reduce your benefit as well—inflation, benefit formulas that discriminate against lower-paid workers in favor of employees in the upper salary brackets, and reduced benefits for workers who are disabled or retire early.

One reason that private pensions are no higher is that they do not change, or very rarely change, with the rising cost of living. One worker wrote: "The original allotments should be guaranteed when inflation gets out of hand and the pension dollar loses its purchasing power. Without these adjustments the pensioner has no way to control the increased cost of living. My pension is $130 a month; my pension allotment has lost $30 of its value [since retirement]. . . . Increased pension rates gained through collective bargaining should be automatically and immediately extended to already retired employees."

Unfortunately, the benefit for most retired pensioners is fixed as of the date of retirement. It can only decrease in value as the cost of living rises. Recently a possible way for retired pensioners to increase their benefits—through collective bargaining—was denied by the Supreme Court when it ruled that unions do not have legal authority to require management to bargain on benefits for retired employees.[8]

Although benefit levels have increased over the years, inflation has made much of that increase illusory as far as buying power is concerned. In 1970 some 4.7 million people received private pension benefits that totaled 7.4 billion dollars.[9] The average yearly outlay per private pension beneficiary, $1654, had increased 62 percent over 1960 when the average outlay was $1021. But the rise in prices between 1960 and 1970 offset those increases so that in terms of buying power the 1970 benefits were only 25 percent higher than in 1960.[10]

Your benefit is usually based on a percentage of your salary in a particular year. For example, you may earn a pension credit of 1 percent of your salary in 1950. But by the time you receive it in 1970, that credit might be worth .5 percent of the 1950 salary in terms of buying power. Some pension benefits are based on average earnings during the five or ten years immediately before retirement. Most workers earn more during their last years of employment than during their first years, so benefits under this arrangement may be higher than under another. (This will be true only if you have many years of service *as well* as a high salary.) But since you may have to depend on your pension for ten or fifteen years or more after you retire, its value will steadily be eroded through the rising cost of living.

Some pension plans adopt cost-of-living formulas that modify benefits to reflect a specified index of prices such as the Consumer Price Index,[11] but these plans are the rare exception and are effective only when overall benefits are adequate to begin with.

Other plans try to gear portions of the benefits to current price levels through earnings in the stock market. These plans, which are called equity annuity plans, and still number very few, allow participants to put part of the contributions made for them into a special investment fund. The first and largest plan of this kind is operated by the College Retirement Equities Fund (CREF) for participants in college and university retirement plans underwritten by the Teachers Insurance and Annuity Association (TIAA). A participant in the TIAA plan is given the option of allocating to CREF a portion of the contributions made in his or her behalf. (Most people who participate in CREF have allotted 50 percent of contributions to this portion of the retirement program.) These monies may earn higher benefits than those in the fixed benefit part of the plan. On the other hand, when the stock market goes down, participants may get lower benefits.

Plan formulas that base pensions on salary and years of service, as almost all do, eat most hungrily into the benefits of workers who change jobs frequently and those who receive low wages. Even if an employee stays with several companies long enough to qualify for benefits under each plan, which is rarely the case, his benefit for a lifetime of work will be less than the benefit of the worker who earns all his pension credits under one plan or with one company.

Consider the worker who earns benefits under three different plans. First, he is likely to "waste" a few years of work under each plan before he is eligible to participate, years that would have been counted toward a pension if he had worked for only one company. This is his major loss. But his total benefit at retirement will also reflect the years spent under the first plan when his wages and benefit formulas were lower. So far as that plan is concerned, he is unable to take advantage of improved benefit formulas or to base his benefit on his final salary that would measurably improve it.

Frank Davis describes his tortured path through several pension plans in the course of a career and the debilitating effect on his final benefit: "My initial termination at Curtiss Wright Electronics Division came under vested pension rights established with a fifteen-year employment period. Hire by International Telephone & Telegraph in program management on the S.A.C. Communication System made me eligible for pension privileges that terminated when the project was concluded and turned over to the Air Force. Rehire one year later by International Telephone (Marlow Sons Division) to manage a special product line made me eligible for their pension plan again on a retroactive basis. All of this was lost when they sold the product line to a company in the Midwest and I was terminated once again.

"Rehire by Curtiss Wright (Engine Division) was to manage the prototype phase of the 747 Boeing Aircraft Landing Gear. I took this job with the understanding that I would be reinstated in the pension plan back to the period of the original termination under vested rights. They reneged on this later and I received only two years' additional credit to my former pension. My termination came . . . and only two years' severance pay.

"Currently I am employed by the Singer Company. If I remain three more years I may collect a small pension under their five-year eligibility requirement.

"The pension I can take now ($180 a month) is about one-half the amount I would have been eligible for if each of these top-ranking U.S. companies had made good on the pension contracts they offer to make employees stay on the job to collect. Nothing is available to you when they decide to lay off at the conclusion of or sale of a product line."

Thus your pension benefit is going to be smaller if you are laid off frequently or cannot work for certain periods regardless of the cause. Even if you don't forfeit your entire pension under these conditions, you forfeit part of it because you will have fewer years of credited service.

For these reasons, blacks and members of other minority groups and women as well are far more likely to receive small benefits, if any, than white male workers. Statistics show that the duration of these groups' employment is far shorter than is true for the rest of the work force. Their concentration in less skilled jobs makes them more vulnerable to layoff, with loss of pensions or reduction of benefits. Besides, they earn relatively lower wages and therefore get smaller benefits even if they manage to work steadily during most of their lives.

Statistics on women illustrate the way pensions operate as a class, not a mass, retirement system. In 1967 half the unmarried women receiving pensions got annual benefits of $664 or less—$200 less than the median pension for unmarried men and $305 less than that for couples.* One reason is that benefits are usually based on salaries, and women earn an average of 30 percent less than men. At retirement they feel the full impact of discriminatory wage scales and hiring practices. Private pension plans erode women's benefits further by requiring long years of continuous employment. Women are statistically more likely than men to be laid off, leave a job temporarily, or move. They are therefore more likely to lose the years of continuous service necessary to qualify for benefits. A recent survey showed that women of all ages had worked only two-thirds as long in their current jobs as men of the same ages. This was true even for those nearing retirement. Half the women between ages sixty and sixty-four had worked only 9.4 years or less in their current jobs; men of the same age had worked a median 15.1 years.[12]

Significantly, industries with the greatest percentage of women workers often have the least satisfactory wage and pension arrangements. In the past these companies and others have often taken advantage of provisions that "allowed" women to retire early in order to force them to retire early and take a reduced benefit. This unfair practice has now been declared illegal by the Supreme Court.

In all these ways,** private pensions have contributed and continue to contribute to the fact that women over sixty-five

---

* Social Security payments to women are also considerably lower than those for men. Median Social Security benefits in 1967 were $860 for unmarried women, $1080 for unmarried men and $1555 for couples.
** The worst form of discrimination against women by private pension plans is their lack of benefits for widows, which will be discussed in the following chapter.

are the poorest segment of our society, with nearly half living below or near the level of poverty.

From the less than $1500 a year that most people get from private pensions, look at the other end of the scale to the huge pension benefits paid to top executives. The following list is taken from corporation proxy statements and includes only pension benefits; additional retirement benefits such as those from stock option programs are not included.

J. K. Jamieson, chairman of the board of Standard Oil Company, Inc., will receive a minimum of $96,000 annual pension and may receive as much as $208,000 a year depending on length of employment and average salary at retirement. James P. McFarland, chairman of the board of General Mills Corporation, will receive at least $100,000 annual pension and possibly more depending on length of employment with the company and average salary at retirement. H. I. Romnes, chairman of the board of AT&T, will receive an annual benefit of $135,570. Paul Thayer, chairman of the board of LTV and LTV Aerospace Corporation, will receive $103,041 annual pension. Roy V. Edwards, president of Wilson & Company, Inc., a subsidiary of LTV, and a member of the board of directors of LTV, will receive $131,712 annual pension. John J. Powers, Jr., chairman of the board of Pfizer, will receive an estimated $85,000 annual pension. Lee Iacocca, president of Ford Motor Company, will get at least $50,000 annual pension and possibly more than $100,000 depending on length of employment and average salary at retirement. James Roche, recently retired chairman of the board of General Motors Corporation, will receive $50,000 annual pension.

The majority of private pension plans compute benefits in conjunction with Social Security benefits. Under this kind of benefit formula (called "integration"), a pension plan promises to pay you a certain percentage of your salary with a benefit comprised *both* of Social Security payments and pensions. Let us say the plan guarantees employees a benefit equal to 50 percent of their salary at retirement. A person making $50,000 a year would qualify for a combined benefit (Social Security plus pension) of $25,000 a year. Very little of this would come from Social Security, which covers only the first portion of an employee's salary (now set at $9000). Almost all of that benefit would have to come from the pension fund. On the other hand, a person making $5000 a year at retirement and eligible for an annual benefit of $2500 would get almost all of his retirement benefit from Social Security; he would actually get very little, if anything, from the private pension fund. If the higher-paid employee were not taking such a large chunk out of the pension fund, more money would be available to raise the benefits of lower-paid workers who are sharing the fund's monies to a lesser extent, although their need is obviously greater.*

I.R.S. regulations do not allow private pension plans to discriminate in favor of one group of employees as opposed to another group under the plan. For example, a plan is not supposed to give benefits only to executives and not to other employees who are also included in the plan and expect ben-

---

* Private pension plans may be set up to cover *only* employees whose salaries are higher than the Social Security base. The theory is that higher paid employees are discriminated against since the employer is not allowed to contribute to Social Security for *all* of their salary, whereas the employer's contributions to Social Security must cover all of the salaries of workers making less than $9000. Therefore, Internal Revenue Service regulations allow employers to contribute to a private pension plan solely for higher-paid employees. The only limitation is that the employer can contribute no more than $37\frac{1}{2}$ percent of an employee's salary above the Social Security base. Thus for a person making $19,000 a year, of which $9000 is covered by Social Security, the employer could make contributions of no more than $3750 ($37\frac{1}{2}$ percent of $10,000). Such theories and regulations have helped the private pension system to become a vehicle for securing the retirement of those most able to provide for themselves, rather than of those least able to support themselves in retirement.

efits. To be approved for tax-exempt status, a private pension plan must appear to be nondiscriminatory.

There are two reasons that this provision may not protect you if you are a lower-wage employee. First, the I.R.S. probably won't discover if your plan does discriminate in favor of executives or some other group. The I.R.S. does not routinely inspect plans for discrimination after they are in operation. Even when the I.R.S. does conduct a tax audit, discriminatory practices may or may not appear.

Second, *some* discrimination may be permissible, especially in plans covering small groups of employees. In these plans, the likelihood is that a substantial shift of benefits from low-pay employees occurs because the managerial employees tend to stay with the company while the low-pay people tend to turn over rapidly, thereby forfeiting their pensions or getting smaller benefits. By and large, the courts have not ruled that such plans violate the I.R.S. regulations against discrimination.

In one case that has set the rule for judging discrimination, the Ryan Aviation pension fund in 1944 covered four officers, one supervisory employee, and 115 other employees. By late 1951, when the plan's operation came to the attention of the I.R.S., the plan had ten participants: five officers, three of the original 115 employees and two newer employees. Of the $71,000 in the pension fund, $52,000 was credited to the accounts of the five officers. This plan was obviously paying off primarily to officers of the corporation, but the court held that it was not "discriminatory." [13]

If a plan is found to violate I.R.S. regulations, the only result is removal of the plan's tax-exempt status. Ironically this "penalty" penalizes only the plan participants. They suffer if the plan is abandoned. They also suffer if it is continued, since the taxes on the pension fund for the entire period may have to come out of the fund itself, that is, out of their money. In either case, participants who lose benefits because of discrimination receive no relief in the form of benefits or anything else.

You will almost certainly get less from your pension fund if you retire early or become disabled. In the 764 plans studied by the Senate Labor Subcommittee, the median monthly payment for normal retirement was $99; for early retirement, $72; and for disability retirement, less than $50.[14]

Some employees do not realize that their benefits will be cut if they retire early. One man worked as a correspondent and editor for the Associated Press for twenty-six years. He decided to take his early retirement option when he was fifty-six, not realizing that he was giving up considerable sums of money to do so. "Had I worked to age sixty-five," he wrote, "I would have received over $400 a month pension. Instead, my pension for twenty-six years of service is a miserable $89.20 per month."

Another employee wrote: "After 32 years of dedicated faithful service for a company in New York, health reasons forced me to retire at sixty-two instead of sixty-five. My benefits were cut considerably. Had I stayed the additional three years I would have drawn $180 instead of $83.88 per month, which I presently receive. This seems most inequitable."

This kind of financial penalty often means that early retirement is not an option for many workers, even when their health or other reasons would make it desirable for them to retire before the age of sixty-five. One woman expressed this view of early retirement when she said: "When I see how I count each day I keep working at my age, I sincerely think some people would retire at sixty if their pension would not be reduced. Factory work is rather hard on the health."

Some pension plans could afford to pay larger benefits to their participants, as well as to give benefits to more participants. For example, the Senate Labor Subcommittee has reported the case of the Kendall Company, which has $5,300,000 in its fund with which to pay benefits and only $1,800,000 in benefit claims.[15] Yet the plan pays an average monthly benefit of only $29.96. The Kendall pension plan has no vesting provisions by which participants can earn benefit rights before they retire, which means that many people are forfeiting their pensions. The money returned to the fund could be used to pay higher benefits, or to pay benefits to more people. Instead it is used to keep company contributions low.

Even if your pension fund does not have large amounts of money left over after all benefit claims are considered, it may be that because of the practices discussed in this chapter, benefits are lower than they need to be.

1. Is your plan paying proportionately larger sums to officers of the company or other high-paid employees? If so, you may want to seek a ruling from the Internal Revenue Service on discrimination.
2. Are your benefits geared to Social Security payments, and if so does this mean the fund is paying more to higher-paid than to lower-paid employees? (This is almost certainly the result in such cases.) If so, you may wish to seek a different benefit formula through your union or personnel manager.
3. Does high turnover among lower-wage employees mean that pensions are going mainly to managerial employees with large salaries who tend to stay with the company? If so, better vesting provisions could give you a more equal share in the fund.

4. Does your plan have provisions for raising benefits according to rising prices to offset inflation?
5. How much will your pension be cut if you take early retirement? If you become disabled?

X

The Public Stake

Millions of Americans are not covered by private pension plans and never expect to be. Why should they be interested in the private pension system? Aren't private pensions of concern only to people who hope to get benefits? Certainly people who are enrolled in private pension plans are most directly affected. But everyone has a stake in how well private pensions serve as a source of retirement income in our country. When private pensions fall short of covering large segments of the private labor force, when they fail to pay off to millions of workers who are covered, when they exclude the widows of deceased workers, when the benefits from private pensions are meager, everyone is involved in taking up the slack. All of us must support welfare programs for the elderly and a larger Social Security program; all of us must bear the social implications of a retired population without the resources to live decently; all of us share the cost of the private pension system—the tax subsidies, the increased consumer costs, and the investment impact of pension funds.

Since private pensions first appeared and began to grow during the 1950's, the theory evolved that there are three sources of retirement income in this country: Social Security, personal savings, and pensions. Economists like to refer to the American system of retirement as a three-legged stool or three-layer cake, though as one writer has pointed out, "The pitiful nature of the income received by most older people from all sources made the analogy of the cake seem something of a mockery." [1]

Nine of every ten American workers can count on Social Security when they retire. But Social Security benefits provide no more than a *bare subsistence* for those who have nothing else to live on. The monthly average benefits for a retired worker in December 1971 was only $132.16.[2]

Personal savings as a source of retirement income are out of reach for most people. Most people just don't have the money to save during their working years. As one congressional task force concluded: "If past performance is a guide, private savings cannot be expected to contribute significantly to raising the level of income in old age. The earning levels leave only *a small excess of income over consumption expenditures* for most families during worklife." [3]

That leaves pensions as many people's last hope for more than the bare subsistence they can expect from Social Security. Yet private pensions cover only half and perhaps less of the private work force. Figures on coverage are confusing. A U.S. Bureau of Labor Statistics survey in 1968 showed that 58 percent of the workers in the private nonfarm economy were "employed in establishments with expenditures for retirement plans." [4] However, a more recent analysis showed that certain employees in these firms were not included in the pension plans: expenditures were being made for some but not all workers. For example, a company might provide a plan for wage but not salary workers, or the reverse. One government economist has concluded that "a substantial majority of the workers in the private sector are not participating in private retirement plans." [5]

Who is covered by the private pension system? By and large, it is the worker who is earning relatively high wages, works for a large, well-established company, and belongs to a union.

Who is not covered? Most likely, this is the worker in a small business who is not earning much money and does not have union representation. The uncovered worker is also likely to be black, or a member of another minority group, or a woman.

A substantial number of people excluded from pensions are unemployed, unpaid family workers, and agricultural workers. But two-thirds of the 30 million or more people in the private nonfarm work force who are without coverage are not in these groups: they are wage and salary workers.[6]

Most of the active workers enrolled in private pension plans—about 60 percent—are employed in manufacturing firms.[7] Another 20 to 25 percent are in transportation, public utilities, and mining. It is estimated that from half to two-thirds of the workers in these areas of employment are covered.[8] The construction and communications industries also have significant coverage.

In contrast to the broad coverage in the manufacturing sector of private industry, pension coverage is sparse in the wholesale and retail trades and service industries. Probably fewer than one-fifth of the workers in these industries are covered.[9]

Emerson Beier of the Bureau of Labor Statistics, in a report published in July 1971, documented the fact that workers without retirement plans are likely to be lower-paid nonunionized employees of small companies.[10] He concluded that "workers who are employed in small nonunion establishments at relatively low levels of pay are the least likely to be participating in a retirement plan. Rapid improvement is effectively blocked by the poor economic position of many small firms. This situation is a matter of serious concern because these workers are among those least able to provide for themselves in later years." [11] In other words, these workers are most likely to become welfare cases when they are old, requiring public assistance at heavy cost to all taxpayers.

Why do so few small businesses offer pension plans? [12] In the main because private pensions appear to operate best with large numbers of both dollars and participants. First, plans for small groups have proportionately high administrative costs. Second, small groups mean a small fund, since contributions are made for relatively fewer employees. Small funds tend to have a lower rate of return so that proportionately more of the cost of benefits is borne by the employer and less by earnings. Third, the mortality rate of small companies is extremely high, so pension plans, where they exist for small groups, are more vulnerable to termination than those in larger, better-established firms.

Another factor is that service enterprises are usually low-skill, low-wage employers who do not compete with other firms on the basis of fringe benefits, especially pensions. Employees in these companies frequently are not unionized or are in weak bargaining positions, so the pressures for pensions in these small enterprises are less than in larger industries.

Prior to 1963 self-employed people (proprietors or partners who own their own businesses) could not set up pension plans that qualified for tax-exemption, with the result that few owner-employers established pension plans for their employees. After enactment of the Self-Employed Retirement Act in 1963, and more particularly, after full tax incentives were granted in 1967, more self-employed persons established retirement programs.[13] However, most of the self-employed who have brought themselves under pension coverage have no full-time employees meeting the requirements for mandatory coverage (three or more years of service).[14] Thus, while the self-employed now face no exclusion from private pension coverage, the new incentives are not succeeding in providing pensions for employees of noncorporate (proprietary or partnership) businesses. Employees of these businesses, usually with low wages and high job turnover, are still effectively shut out of a source of retirement income to supplement Social Security.

Many private pension plans provide nothing for widows of covered workers; no plan provides more than a pittance. This failure is one of the system's greatest shortcomings as an answer to our nation's retirement problems. Better provisions for widows under private pension plans would help solve one of the most pressing needs of the over-sixty-five population—the lack of income for older women. Older widows and women over sixty-five who live alone comprise the poorest segment of our population. Six out of every ten have incomes below the poverty level.[15]

The importance of providing for widows of covered workers was underlined by a recent survey of United Auto Workers Union members and their survivors; the survey revealed that without pension benefits most survivors would be virtually destitute. About 75 percent of the surveyed UAW families had financial resources at the worker's death of less than $3000.[16]

Most retired workers assume that if they die their widows

will continue to receive their pensions; most active workers believe their wives will get a benefit from their plan if they die. Most are wrong. Many pension plans make no provisions at all for widows or other dependents.* Even under plans that do provide a survivors' benefit, it usually goes to widows only under certain conditions and only if the husband has followed certain complicated procedures. In these instances, widows often receive nothing because of the numerous technicalities surrounding the survivors' benefit option. Thousands of widows have found themselves unexpectedly without pension support. Some of them have written:

"My husband died in 1970 while still working for the same company [he had worked for] for thirty-one years. The company said I would not get a nickel of his pension because my name was not on a certain paper."

"I was one of those unfortunate widows who could not collect on my husband's pension plan. My husband was within two months of collecting his first pension check when he passed away."

"The company doesn't want to pay me my husband's pension. They say if they had been paying his pension when he died they would have paid it to me. I think they should pay it to me as he was killed in their company."

". . . my husband had asked in a letter how I would stand [in the pension plan] in case of his death. This question was ignored and when he passed away I was told that he should

---

* A study by the Bureau of Labor Statistics of private pension plans under collective bargaining in 1962 found that only one-half of the plans surveyed even allowed workers the option of providing for their widows, usually by giving up part of their benefit while they live. Even fewer nonbargained plans, those offered unilaterally by employers, include survivors benefit options. Fewer plans still have automatic death benefits: a 1968 B.L.S. study of one hundred selected plans—mostly large plans with relatively liberal provisions—found only forty-four with automatic death benefits.

have made these arrangements three years before he retired."

Most plans with survivors' benefit provisions merely offer employees the option of giving up part of their pension in order that their widows may get something.[17] For example, if your pension benefit is $100 a month, you could agree to take $80 a month so that your wife can receive $40 a month if you die. To give a widow a benefit equal to the full amount of the reduced benefit, most worker's pensions are reduced by about one-third. Even then, the option might apply only if the employee is already retired when he dies, or under other plans, only if he is still working at time of death. In any case the employee has to exercise the option through application to the plan administrator or the union, often several years before expected retirement date. Numbers of employees do not know about these options or don't know about the procedures they must follow to exercise the option. Others put it off until too late. Some simply don't want to take a reduced benefit or can't afford to since the full benefit is often so small. Many consider the widow's benefit too meager to be worth the trouble. For various reasons few workers exercise the survivors' option.[18] One large plan reported several years ago that not a single retiring worker elected the option.[19]

The kind of survivors' benefit option where the worker chooses to take a cut in his own benefit in order to pay something to his widow costs the employer nothing extra.[20] The employee is essentially paying for the widow's benefit out of his own benefit. In 1962, the United Auto Workers Union negotiated a survivors benefit in its bargained pension plans that provided for employers to contribute. The retired employee still took a reduced benefit, but the employer also helped pay for the widow's benefit. For example, an employee who was entitled to a pension of $100 a month could get $90 while he lived and $45 went to his widow if he died. Since that time UAW plans have added a two-year benefit for widows of employees who die while still working. Widows over fifty may receive a small benefit until they reach age sixty-two and become entitled to Social Security. At that time the pension payments stop. Ironically, these severely limited provisions for widows and dependents are considered liberal in the private pension industry.

Automatic death benefits, not surprisingly, are even more limited and found less often. James Schulz has reported that the most common kind of automatic death benefit is a monthly payment to the survivor for a six-month to five-year period. After that, benefits cease entirely, although, as Schulz points out, "the survivors' living expenses continue and no doubt increase over time." [21]

Another automatic survivors' benefit is found in plans where employees contribute to the fund. The survivors' benefit merely returns the employee's contribution to the survivor along with interest (usually two to three percent).

The third most common automatic survivors' benefit is a lump-sum payment of $1000 to $3500.

The least common type of automatic death benefit, according to Schulz, gives the survivor a percentage of the normal retirement benefit of the retiree. These benefits are usually reduced if any previous benefits have been paid to the retiree before his death.

Employers object primarily to the expense of survivors' benefits. They also point to the group life insurance, which many companies provide for their employees. In most cases, however, insurance plans pay a lump sum to survivors, rarely amounting to more than a year or two of the deceased employee's salary. Insurance does not take the place of a monthly income stretched over the lifetime of the survivor. Besides, insurance coverage stops when the worker retires; if he dies a year later, his widow has nothing.

On their side, unions have applied little pressure to include survivors' benefits in pension plans. A few multiemployer plans offer survivors' options, including teamsters and packing house workers among others. The UAW has been uniquely active in this area.

Survivors' benefits have not been part of the pension debate in Congress and the Federal government. Alone among all of the major issues, this one has hardly even been raised. It was not mentioned in the report of the President's Committee on Corporate Pension Funds in 1965, or in Nelson McClung's survey article on old age income assurance for the Joint Economic Committee in 1966, or in the report of the President's Task Force on Aging in 1970, or in the income recommendations of the White House Conference on Aging in 1971.

Few other areas of private pension reform are more needful of action from employees. The place to begin is with your own plan:

1. Does your plan include a survivors benefit? If not, you may want to press your union to give this issue priority in negotiating a new contract or press your employer to provide benefits to widows. You may wish to point out that the company employs not only the individual but the family unit as well, a fact already recognized in the area of health benefits, which generally cover the employee and his or her dependents.
2. If your plan does offer a survivors option, does it apply if you die before you retire? After you retire?
3. Does the benefit go to the widow only until she is eligible for Social Security? Or only for a fixed number of years?

4. How much of a reduction must you take in your pension in order to provide for your survivors in case of death? If the reduction is sizeable, that means the survivors benefits are probably costing the employer little or no additional contributions. You may want to press the employer to help share the cost with you and your fellow employees.
5. Have you exercised the survivors option properly?
6. How much will your survivor get?

The three-legged stool theory of retirement income (Social Security, personal savings, pension) was based on the expectation that private pensions would continue to increase their coverage as well as their actual pay-off. But during the 1960's there has been a marked slowdown in the number of employees coming under private pension coverage. Although approximately 10 million workers were added to the rolls of private pension plans during the past decade, about 1 million a year, for the first time the rate of added coverage is now less than the rate of growth of the entire labor force. In addition, most of the added coverage resulted from increased employment in firms already offering plans. New plans covering workers previously without coverage grew at a much slower rate.

In the early 1960's, certain economists were predicting that by 1980 from 30 to 40 percent of all people over 65 would be receiving pension payments. Today those predictions are less certain. Some people are cautioning that only 20 percent of the population over 65 will ever benefit from the private pension system as it exists today. Some people are saying that we should shift our resources to greater support of the Social Security system.

A Joint Economic Committee report has reluctantly concluded: "There is no real likelihood in the foreseeable future . . . that a majority of older people will become eligible for supplemental pensions. Too much of the problem of income maintenance for old age is a problem of survivors' insurance for widows, which is seldom covered by private pension plans; too many jobs are difficult to include in private pension plans; and very early vesting would be required to supply protection to the large numbers of workers that change jobs frequently." [22]

How much can we expect private pensions to grow in the future? Have plans already been established in those industries that lend themselves best to pension coverage? Even among those who are covered, will pensions ever be more than a payoff for the lucky few? These are some of the questions that concern everyone.

Furthermore, private pensions play a major role in determining the standard of living that most Americans can expect at retirement whether or not they are covered by a private pension plan or receive a benefit if they are covered. The expectation that private pensions will pay off for some workers reduces the pressure to increase benefits under Social Security. This leaves the person who receives only Social Security worse off than if the private pension did not exist.

Today one-quarter of the people over sixty-five in the United States live in poverty and another 25–30 percent are on the border. Unless they are to be ignored, the public will have to support them. That burden becomes heavier if the private retirement system fails to grow, fails to extend coverage to those now without it (particularly to those least able to provide for retirement through savings, investments, or other means), and fails to provide benefits to so many who are covered.

To the price we are paying for the private pension system must be added the sizeable tax subsidy. In 1971 the private

pension system cost taxpayers more than 3 billion dollars in tax deductions for contributions to pension funds. This meant some 3 billion dollars had to be made up by higher taxes for other taxpayers or by reduced public services.

Then we must add the substantial cost to consumers of higher prices necessary to enable employers to offer private pensions. When the pension benefits go only to a few privileged employees, often the highest paid employees, such consumer costs are questionable. Congresswoman Martha W. Griffiths, D-Michigan, has stated the problem this way: "There are millions of Americans who do not qualify under any private pension plan and the thing that is totally unfair is that those millions are buying ten million cars a year for which they are paying a price that covers a pension of $500 a month or approximately that for an auto worker. . . . It seems to me that if we are going to have pensions that the pension system has to work for everybody. . . ."[23]

Everyone is affected, too, by the impact of private pension funds on the economy. An important impact is the reduction in labor mobility. When workers are tied to their jobs through fear of pension loss, not only do they lose an essential freedom, the rest of us also pay the consequences of a more static labor force: declining industries supported by captive workers; new and promising industries held back because prospective workers are not free to change jobs; development of geographic and industrial areas determined by the contingencies of pension funds rather than by the demands of the economy.

Another economic impact of private pension funds is their huge concentration of economic power. During 1971, for example, private pension funds made gross purchases of 21.7 billion dollars in common stock, more than the common stock purchases of mutual funds. Net purchases, that is, gross purchases minus gross sales, of private pension funds amounted to an astounding 8.9 billion dollars.[24] Whoever controls the sale and purchases of stocks for private pension funds obviously wields enormous power in our corporate structure.

Two-thirds of all private pension funds are managed by bank trust departments, with a handful of banks getting the lion's share. For most of these fund assets, banks have sole power to make investments and vote their shares.[25] The growth of bank decision-making power has grown particularly among the largest banks. The four largest bank trust departments in the country hold 43 percent of all pension plan assets in trust departments; the ten largest banks account for 58 percent; and the twenty largest have 72 percent.[26] This means that through pension fund accounts, a relatively small number of banks have accumulated control over significant amounts of stock in a major segment of large American corporations. The investment lists of these major banks tend to favor the larger companies, further concentrating bank influence over an important segment of the economy of the United States.

The result of ever increasing stock control by banks through their growing pension accounts has been to add more weight to corporate-management interests as opposed to public or stockholder interests. Almost one-fifth of the major bank trust departments have a policy of always voting for management, according to one study.[27] This policy—a trend even where it does not exist as specific dictum—measurably reduces the opportunities for challenging corporate decision-making. Greater concern in proxy voting for the interests of beneficiaries of pension funds might increase the possibilities for injecting other points of view.

Still another result of the growing private pension industry is the increased possibility of conflicts of interest that can affect other stockholders and the public. At the heart of this problem is the close association among directors of banks, corporations, and pension funds—"interlocking directorships." There are few safeguards against the sharing of confidential information through which certain interests may be furthered to the exclusion of others.

A classic example of what can happen when such interests interlock around a pension fund is the trading of Penn Central stock shortly before the announcement of the railroad's bankruptcy.[28] Between April 1, 1970, and June 21, 1970 (when the railroad's bankruptcy was made public), there were heavy sales of Penn Central stock by Chase Manhattan National Bank and other financial institutions. Chase Manhattan was a major creditor of Penn Central. At the time of the bankruptcy, the bank held 50 million dollars of the outstanding debt of the railroad and its various subsidiaries. In addition, in June 1970, Penn Central and its subsidiaries had 5 million dollars on deposit at Chase Manhattan. The bank was also a member of the bank steering committee that was trying to participate in a proposed government guaranteed loan to Penn Central.

Finally, the president of the railroad, Stuart Saunders, was a member of the board of directors of Chase Manhattan throughout the period of the stock trading.

Similar ties existed between the railroad and three other banking institutions that also sold Penn Central stock shortly before the public was aware of the bankruptcy. These were Morgan Guaranty Trust Company, Continental Illinois National Bank and Trust Company, and the Allegheny group, which included the Investors Mutual, Inc., and Investors Diversified Services. During the weeks before bankruptcy was announced, these four institutions together sold 1,751,225 shares of Penn Central stock, almost one-third of all the Penn Central stock sold during the period.

Almost all of the shares of Penn Central stock sold by Chase

Manhattan came from the bank's discretionary trust accounts, largely pension funds. Practically no sales were made from nondiscretionary trust accounts. Representative Wright Patman, D-Texas, chairman of the House Banking and Currency Committee, noted: "It becomes apparent that the trust departments of such banking institutions as Chase Manhattan conducted their massive sales of Penn Central stock on the basis of either great clairvoyance or inside information." [29]

The Penn Central case illustrates the way in which the public, in this case particularly other stockholders, can be affected by information-sharing and use of inside information in handling the large amounts of stock in private pension funds.

Pension plan participants are affected by the concentration of control of their monies in a few financial institutions; the public is equally affected when this concentration furthers the interests of private corporations to the virtual neglect of the public interest. Greater disclosure of investments to plan participants and the public and the limiting of interlocking directorships would be a beginning toward diversifying the unprecedented concentration of economic power through management of pension funds.

Certainly it is time to realize that all Americans pay the price of supporting the private pension system, a price which may be higher than is justified by the limited benefit of pensions today. Proposals for reform, therefore, should be of concern not only to those most directly affected—people now participating in private pension plans—but also to (1) those in the private labor force who are excluded from the private pension system; (2) taxpayers who support welfare and other programs to help the large numbers of retired people with inadequate incomes; (3) recipients of Social Security whose benefits may be reduced because an elite number of the work force can sup-

THE PUBLIC STAKE 107

plement Social Security with private pensions; (4) stockholders who are at a disadvantage competing with banks and other financial institutions that manage large blocks of private pension fund investments; (5) the public whose interests are rarely reflected in the purchase, sale, and voting of pension fund stockholdings.

XI

Revising the Rules

Proposals are being considered by the Congress that would correct parts of the private pension system. You should make sure you know what these proposals are and support those you believe will lead to greater security for you.

The most comprehensive pension bills are those introduced by Senators Harrison Williams, D-New Jersey, and Jacob Javits, R-New York (S. 3598); by Representative John H. Dent, D-Pennsylvania (H.R. 1269). The Nixon administration's vesting and other benefit proposals are contained in H.R. 12272, introduced by Representative Wilbur Mills, D-Arkansas, chairman of the House Ways and Means Committee. The President has also proposed fiduciary standards for pension plan administrators in H.R. 12337, introduced by Representative John N. Erlenborn, R-Illinois. Bill numbers refer to the 92nd Congress.

These three legislative packages will be discussed in this chapter. (For a summary of other proposed pension legislation, see Appendix B.)

Vesting

All the major legislative proposals include requirements for giving employees certain pension rights before they retire.

The Williams-Javits bill would require full vesting of pension credits within fifteen years after an employee enters employment under the plan. After eight years of service, 30 percent of the credits earned up to that time would become nonforfeitable even if the employee leaves the company. Each year thereafter, another 10 percent would become nonforfeitable until, after fifteen years of service, the employee has a right to all his credits. (This is known as graded vesting.)

(It should be noted here that Senator Javits' original bill (S. 2) provided for vesting of 10 percent of credits after six years, with full vesting after fifteen years of service. Changes in this and other provisions were made in an effort to come up with a "bill designed to pass," according to the Senator's aides. In assessing the bill—or any piece of legislation—employees should be wary of compromises that are against their interests.)

The Dent bill would require full vesting of all earned benefits within ten years of service after the employee reached age twenty-five.

The major difference between the two bills is that, under the Williams-Javits proposal, a worker could gain partial benefit rights after eight years of service but would not have full rights until he had worked for fifteen years. Under the Dent bill, an employee might have no rights for ten years, but after that time, all of his credits would become nonforfeitable.

The Williams-Javits bill, unlike the Dent bill, would provide for vesting based on aggregate years of service rather than continuous service, thus eliminating the break-in-service requirement that deprives many employees of their pensions. The Dent bill would authorize the Secretary of Labor to decide whether break-in-service rules are reasonable.

President Nixon has proposed the "rule of 50" as a vesting requirement. Under this guideline half of an employee's benefits would become nonforfeitable when his age plus his years of service equalled fifty. For example, an employee could gain the right to half his benefits at age forty with ten years of service (age forty plus ten years of service = fifty). An additional 10 percent of his pension would become nonforfeitable every year thereafter until the entire pension was vested. This, of course, would help fewer employees attain vested rights than would the Dent or Williams-Javits proposals. The President's proposals in all respects are more limited than the other bills, which, however, also contain serious limitations.

Portability

Related to vesting are proposals that would allow employees to take their pension credits with them when they changed jobs. For credits to be portable they must be vested, that is, nonforfeitable; so portability has little meaning without early vesting requirements.

The Williams-Javits bill would set up a voluntary system under which employers operating pension plans (or profit-sharing retirement plans) could transfer the money contributed for an employee who left the plan to a portability fund administered by the Secretary of Labor. The transferred money would be credited to the individual's account in a special fund. It would later be paid over to a new plan that the employee joined, if the plan were similar to the old one, or it would remain in the special fund and benefits would be paid to the employee when he retired or to his beneficiaries if he died.

The Dent bill would direct the Secretary of Labor to study portability, including the problems of reciprocity among various types of plans and various benefit levels.

The Nixon administration has made no proposals relating to portability.

Funding

Funding proposals would set regulations aimed at making sure pension funds have enough money to pay off a certain number of claims at all times, and after a period of time, to pay *all* claims earned under the plan.

Under the Williams-Javits bill, pension plans would have to have enough money to cover all credits earned under the plan, whether vested or not, within thirty years. If a plan terminated, the employer would be liable to pay all claims that should be covered according to the funding schedule. The bill would permit the exemption of multiemployer plans that enrolled at least 25 percent of the employees in their industry, either nationally or within a particular area, if no single employer employed more than one-fifth of the participants in the plan and if conditions in the industry were such that a substantial decrease in employment was unlikely.

The Dent bill would require that pension plans maintain a certain funding schedule to cover increasing amounts of the vested rights earned under the plan. Within twenty-five years plans would be required to have enough money to cover all vested benefits. Failure to meet the funding requirements would mean that benefits could not be increased until the proper amount of money was contributed. The plan administrator would also have to inform employees with vested benefit rights of benefits that could not be paid if the plan terminated.

The major difference between the two bills is that the Williams-Javits proposal would require funding of all credits whether vested or not, while the Dent bill would require funding only of nonforfeitable claims.

President Nixon has offered no funding proposals.

Reinsurance

Mandatory insurance programs are proposed in both the Williams-Javits and the Dent bills. The Williams-Javits bill would require that all pension plans approved for tax exemption be insured under a program administered by the Secretary of Labor. An individual's vested pension rights would be insured up to $500 a month or half the average monthly wage during the five years of highest wages, whichever is less. Vested benefits would be protected, for example, if a company or unit closed down and the pension plan did not have enough money to pay all claims.

Under the Dent bill an insuring corporation would be established in the U.S. Department of Labor. If the plans met the required funding ratio, 90 percent of the claims that were not covered by money in the fund would be insured. That is, if the funding regulations required a plan to have enough money to cover twenty percent of the claims, nine-tenths of the remaining 80 percent of claims would be protected by insurance. If the plan had not met its proper funding ratio, the insurance would cover a smaller part of the difference.

President Nixon made no proposals for reinsurance. Referring to a lack of data on workers affected by plan terminations, Mr. Nixon directed the Departments of Treasury and Labor to study terminations "to determine what federal policy should be on questions such as funding, the nature of the employer's liability and termination insurance."

Fiduciary rules

Requirements that would hold pension fund trustees more strictly accountable to the beneficiaries of the plan and attempt to prevent misuse of funds have been proposed in the Williams-Javits and Dent bills and in the Employee Benefits Protection Act proposed by the Nixon administration. The most important provisions in all of these proposals are the following:

1. Rules of conduct, virtually identical in all three bills, would be laid down for administrators of pension trusts aimed at holding them accountable exclusively to the beneficiaries.
2. The rules would prohibit trustees from selling, purchasing, or lending pension monies to "known parties in interest." These would include officials of the pension plan, or persons providing services to the plan, or employers whose employees are covered by the plan.
3. The administrator would also be prohibited from using pension funds in his own interests or receiving compensation from other parties in connection with fund transactions.
4. The pension fund administrator would be personally liable for making good losses caused by breaches of fiduciary responsibilities. The administrator would also be required to restore to the fund any profits he earned through use of assets of the fund.
5. Investments in securities issued by the employer would be limited to 10 percent of the market value of the fund's as-

sets. Exempt from this requirement would be profit-sharing, stock bonus, and thrift and savings plans.
6. Broader disclosure provisions would include:
—Clear and simple descriptions of pension plans for employees.
—Annual pension plan reports to plan participants. (All three bills require that complete annual reports be furnished to participants on request. The Dent bill requires that summaries of annual reports, as well as plan descriptions, be furnished automatically to all participants.)
—Annual audits of pension funds.
—A listing in the annual pension report of each investment, purchase, loan, or other financial transaction exceeding $100,000 or 3 percent of the value of the pension plan's assets.
—Identification in the annual reports of loans in default, or written off as uncollectible, and leases in default.
—Detailed listing and information in the reports about transactions with interested parties.
—Statements in the reports of the present value of all vested benefits and other liabilities; the ratio of market value of assets to liabilities; the number of participants discharged during the year; their vested rights, if any, and length of service; the present value of their vested benefits and value of forfeited benefits.
7. Lawsuits to enforce these fiduciary responsibilities could be brought through civil actions filed in Federal or state courts. Actions to enjoin violations could be brought by the Secretary of Labor. Federal officials and participants could bring actions to recover benefits and redress of grievances. For willful violations the Williams-Javits and Nixon bills provide criminal penalties of a fine not exceeding $1000 and/or imprisonment of not more than six

months. The Dent bill provides a fine of up to $10,000 and a maximum prison term of five years.

Special provisions in the three bills include the following:
1. *Coverage.* Coverage of the new fiduciary responsibilities and disclosure requirements proposed by the Williams-Javits and Nixon bills would be essentially the same as under the present disclosure laws, applying to pension plans with twenty-six or more participants. The Dent bill would cover plans with nine or more participants.
2. *Information to employees.* The Nixon and Dent bills would require the administrator to furnish terminating employees with statements of their vested benefit rights; similar information would be available for all current participants on request. The Dent bill would require that this information also be reported to the Secretary of Health, Education and Welfare for use in notifying individuals of their eligibility for benefits.
3. President Nixon has proposed legislative action (H.R. 12272) to allow employees who wish to save for their own retirement to deduct from their income tax amounts set aside for a pension program. An individual could deduct up to $1500 a year, or 20 percent of his income, whichever is less. Taxes would also be deferred on earnings from those investments. (An individual who began annual investments of $1500 at age forty would have an annual pension of $7500 at age sixty-five. If he began investing at age fifty, he would have $3375 a year at age sixty-five; beginning at age sixty, $900.)
4. Mr. Nixon also proposed a higher amount of tax-deductible investments for pension savings for self-employed persons. The self-employed may now invest $2500 a year, or 10 percent of earned income, whichever is less. Under the Nixon proposal, they could make annual deductible con-

tributions of $7500, or 15 percent of income, whichever is less.

5. The Williams-Javits bill would remove all restrictive eligibility rules from pension plans. Plans would be required to admit employees to participation in the plan from the date the employer contributes to the plan on their behalf, and in no event later than six months from the date of hire. The Dent bill permits plans to set eligibility for participation at three years or age twenty-five, whichever is later.

President Nixon would allow an employer to exclude from coverage employees under the age of thirty and those who had not worked for at least three years, whatever their age. The Nixon bill would also allow employers to exclude from coverage employees who first became eligible within five years of the normal retirement age.

6. Prior to the Williams-Javits bill, Senator Javits had introduced S. 2 that called for consolidated enforcement of all laws and regulations governing private pension plans in a newly created central pension commission. However, in the subsequent compromise bill (S. 3598), this provision was dropped. The compromise bill creates a new division within the Department of Labor and a new Assistant Secretary of Labor to enforce the standards and reporting provisions of the bill. Tax law enforcement would remain with the Internal Revenue Service.

7. Another key compromise in the Williams-Javits bill is a "grandfather" provision (section 215) allowing a company to set up a new pension plan complying with the new Act for employees hired after the law goes into effect, while it can, if it wishes, retain the old plan on an optional basis for old employees. The old employees would have the choice to remain with the old plan, which might offer

larger benefits without vesting provisions, or go with the new plan. Senator Javits' aides doubt that any but the oldest workers would choose to remain with the old plans.

Unfortunately these bills have suffered the fate of private pension plans in general: they have been compromised and weakened to meet industry and union demands at the expense of beneficiaries. Although they would improve the chances for some people to get a pension, they do little or nothing for others, and they leave unresolved major weaknesses in the private pension system.

The Williams-Javits bill is the one taken most seriously by those who seek reform. Its limitations may be taken as the measure of how far we are from meaningful proposals for a better system. Merton Bernstein, a leading pension expert, has said that the bill "provides a mirage of reform but not its substance." S. 3598 does nothing to help the more than 30 million Americans in the private labor force who are not covered by a pension plan. It offers no solution to the cost problems that keep many small employers from offering plans to their employees; rather it adds costs to increase their difficulties. The bill's vesting proposals do not help the seasonal worker, the parttime worker, or people who change jobs at intervals of less than eight years. These Americans number in the millions and would continue to be excluded from pension coverage.

Women find little of benefit in the Williams-Javits proposals. Millions of working women will not be able to meet the eight-year minimum service requirement for a right to 30 percent of their pension. Millions of others will continue to work for small employers who do not offer coverage. The bill does nothing for widows, and, in fact, the additional pension costs it would impose could discourage inclusion of survivors benefits. Plan administrators may seek to pay for the bill's added vesting and funding requirements by cutting costs elsewhere; an obvious place to cut is the provision for widows.

The Williams-Javits bill does nothing for employees who lose their benefits through "partial terminations," as when plans terminate because one unit of a multi-unit company is closed down or sold. Existing law goes farther than the bill: current tax regulations provide that the Internal Revenue Service may declare a partial termination so that affected workers would get something from the fund. However, the I.R.S. has been reluctant to implement these regulations. Merton Bernstein suggests that a reform statute should "eliminate uncertainties about the law" and "require 100 percent vesting of all credits when significant units of multi-unit enterprises shut down." [1] In addition, the bill might have included, but does not include, provisions for workers who are separated from their jobs during business declines before their plan is terminated and therefore lose any claim on the monies in the fund.

Many people who are covered by the Williams-Javits vesting provisions would not benefit for years. As first proposed, all employees, no matter how long they have worked, would have to start from the beginning to meet the service requirements. Workers who have already worked eight or more years for their employer would have to work eight more to acquire the service credits for vesting. Then they would have to work an additional year because the bill's vesting requirements would not be effective for a year after passage. The bill was amended in committee to allow workers aged forty-five and older to count credits earned before the bill's passage. But younger workers would not receive vested rights under the Williams-Javits proposal for at least nine years. In addition, multiemployer plans would be allowed to apply for three-year deferrals; for many employees under these plans, the bill would bring no vesting benefits for twelve years. Even when vesting is achieved, only 30 percent of a worker's credits would vest; under multiemployer plans you might not get full vesting for a total of nineteen years, and under single employer plans for at least sixteen years.

The bill provides that plans be fully funded after thirty years. This provision would help only a fraction of the employees who lose benefits because their plans terminate without enough money to pay their benefits. It would not, for example, have prevented the large pension losses in the well-known Studebaker case, where the company plan required thirty-year funding.

Reinsurance provisions in the Williams-Javits bill, providing benefits where funds lack sufficient monies at termination, are limited to vested benefits.

The Williams-Javits bill does little to improve benefit levels under private pensions. An employee would earn a right to 30 percent of his benefit credits after eight years employment (amounting to about 2.4 years' worth). However, these credits would be frozen at their value on the date the employee left the company. If the worker earned them early in his career, these credits would be severely reduced in value by the time he collected them twenty or more years later. Employees who remained in the same job would profit from increased benefit levels reflecting the rising cost of living, while their more mobile colleagues would be penalized for changing jobs.

To avoid loss of pension rights and reduced benefits for mobile workers, the bill proposes a means through which an employee's credits could be transferred from one employer to another. The proposal is of dubious value, however, since the program would be entirely voluntary and so limited in the investments it could make that many employers would avoid it.

The bill leaves enforcement of its provisions to the same

Federal agencies now involved in regulation of private pension plans—the Department of Treasury's Internal Revenue Service, the Securities and Exchange Commission, and the Labor Department, where the bill would create a new assistant secretary. This enforcement procedure is far inferior to the central pension commission first proposed by Senator Javits in his original bill, S. 2. The I.R.S.'s primary concern is enforcing tax laws and increasing revenue, not protecting pension plan participants. The Labor Department is notorious for lax enforcement of regulations under its purview. A central pension commission would have established a one-stop service so that people concerned about any aspect of the pension problem would have to contact only one agency. It would also have concentrated pension expertise in one Federal department, better enabling the Federal government to deal effectively with the powerful and complex private institutions involved in private pension plans. This provision was dropped at the expense of plan participants and in favor of the pension industry, which prefers to see government authority spread loosely over a number of departments.

Having discussed the most liberal pension bill before Congress, we turn to one of the most limited: the Nixon bill. Older workers will find that President Nixon's vesting proposals can work against them. The Nixon rule of fifty (half a worker's pension vests when his age plus years of service equal fifty) means that employers must provide pensions for older workers though not for younger ones. It thus increases the incentive for employers to avoid hiring older people. The rule also means that employers early in a worker's career contribute little or nothing to his pension; most or all of the cost falls on the last employer, again discouraging employers from hiring or retaining older workers.

Merton Bernstein has summed up the criticism of the Nixon

rule of fifty: "Older workers—which may mean over thirty-five—have a difficult enough time without presenting employers and prospective employers with higher pension costs than younger competitors. Despite protestations to the contrary, the rule of 50 would mean higher pension costs for older workers, especially but not exclusively those over 50." [2]

Bernstein and others have pointed out that immediate or early vesting for all workers greatly reduces the disadvantage of hiring older employees.

H.R. 12272, the Administration bill, provides for vesting but not funding standards, raising expectations without providing a necessary means for meeting them. Labor Secretary James Hodgson told the Senate Labor Subcommittee that "we believe funding is the kind of element in a private pension system that is best left to bargainers and employers." Formal funding requirements might, he said, "restrict the growth and vitality of the private pension system." [3]

Most people interested in reforming the system, however, deny that you can implement meaningful improvements while ignoring funding. Senator Harrison Williams has pointed to the recent closing of the Ballantine Brewery in Newark, New Jersey, and noted that "vesting was great but funding was nearly zero. The employees got no benefits in fact." [4]

The Nixon bill simply writes off the worker who is within five years of retirement. Employers could exclude this worker from pension coverage entirely. Further, the bill allows employers to exclude workers from pension coverage until they work at least three years for the company. Thus a new employee aged fifty would have to wait three years before gaining pension rights and since the bill is prospective, he would earn credits only on future work; the bill grants no vested rights for the previous years worked.

President Nixon has appeared especially proud of his proposal to give tax deferrals to people who want to save for their retirement. The administration has billed this provision as an effort to help the more than 30 million employees in the private labor force not covered by pensions. In fact this proposal will help only the well-to-do, a small fraction of those lacking pension coverage; it would do nothing for the average person. An employee need only ask himself how easily he could set aside $1500 a year or 20 percent of his present earnings. (The lesser of the two is the total amount for which a tax deferral could be taken under the Nixon proposal.) Most people cannot save anything, much less $1500 a year. Can a family with an earned income of $5000 a year save $1000, or 20 percent of their income? Can a family with an income of $7500 a year set aside $1500 of that? Even engineers with average incomes of $17,000–$18,000 a year say they would be hard pressed to save $1500. Obviously people earning $30,000 or $50,000 a year would profit significantly from a tax shelter for retirement savings. But the bill does nothing for the people who find it hardest to save for retirement, the very people who need a pension. By purporting to help them, while doing no more than handing another advantage to the wealthy, the Nixon Administration is guilty of serious misrepresentation, or as one labor leader termed it, of supporting "class legislation." [5]

It has been suggested that if these proposals are the best we can do to reform private pensions, we should scrap pensions and try to improve Social Security. Merton Bernstein points out that Social Security "has never lost a penny to a dishonest trustee, never paid a kickback to a union or management official, never failed to pay off for lack of funding, can readily be made to keep up with increases in the cost of living, pays off to widows and children and other dependents when a worker dies, retires, or becomes disabled. In sum, [Social Security] is

REVISING THE RULES   123

dependable where private pensions are undependable. Its weakness is benefits that are too low. But there is no easier, no cheaper, no more dependable way to improve retirement income than through Social Security." [6]

How costly would it be to expand Social Security if at the same time we rid ourselves of the public expense of private pensions, including more than 3 billion dollars tax revenue loss and increased consumer costs of goods and services to help employers pay for pensions? Increasingly, people in Washington —members of Congress and labor unions, government officials, economists, and public interest advocates—are asking, Why the private system? Why not an expansion of Social Security? Even more significantly, there are indications that rank-and-file employees are beginning to see an improved Social Security system, not private pensions, as the better answer to their retirement problems. Out of more than 500 people who answered our questionnaire, when asked whether they would rather see higher Social Security benefits for everyone or more people getting private pensions, only nine more people opted for the private system than for Social Security.

In fact, we do not yet know whether the private pension system can be made to work in the way most people believe it should or whether it is essentially too flawed and too expensive ever to offer more than its present limited benefits. We do not know because we have not yet seriously attempted to improve the system. Up to now, pension legislation has been formulated in the virtual absence of constituent pressure—that is, pressure from employees who hope to benefit from the system. Without their involvement, legislative reforms will continue to do too little. The bills we have discussed in this chapter represent the most farreaching legislative reform efforts to date. Yet they are pitifully weak. How much stronger would they be if congressmen were as familiar with employees' desires as with the desires of employers? How much stronger would they be if beneficiaries conducted even half the lobbying efforts of the pension industry? We do not yet know the answer.

If constituents were more active in their own behalf, the pension industry might also be spurred to look for new innovative ways of improving the system. Certainly the present method of providing private pension benefits is not the only way. Rather than simply patching up the old system, we might create a new framework for private pensions that would not only be feasible but would meet the basic unsolved problems of the present approach: a system that would cover all or nearly all employees in the private sector; that would allow workers to earn pension benefits for every year they work no matter how often they change jobs; that would fund all credits in full; that would protect the fiduciary interests of employees by taking the management of pension funds out of the hands of employers and unions; that would prevent unhealthy concentration of economic power and allow employees to have a voice in pension investment policies.

Such a private pension system is entirely possible. The first step would be creation of private independent pension funds outside the control of employers and unions. Each employee could choose a fund where he would set up a pension account. Employers would contribute to these pension funds for their employees rather than to company plans and would receive the same tax deductions for their contributions. Employees would have passbooks to keep track of the total amount in their accounts. They could also contribute their own money to their retirement accounts if they wished, with a tax deduction. The contributions made for all employees would vest immediately. If employees changed jobs, the new employer would begin making contributions to their account. Their pension money would not be endangered if their company became insolvent, or sold to another firm, or closed down their plant.

An employee would receive a lifetime annuity beginning at any time he chose to file a declaration of retirement (but only one time during his life). The amount of the annuity would be determined by the total amount in his account divided by his life expectancy plus cost of living adjustments. The funds would be insured and provide benefits to dependent surviving spouses.

This system would cost employers no more than they are currently paying to pension funds because the earnings on contributions to an employee's benefit spread over an entire work life would be much greater than when the benefit is funded only during the last ten or fifteen years of the employee's career, as it is now. Yet the average employee would be far better off. Average benefits would be higher and more employees would be covered. So that workers now covered by a pension plan would get what they have been promised, while new young employees benefit from the new system, there would be a transition period.

Employees would participate in the management of their retirement funds in that fund directors would be elected by fund members. Officers would be appointed by the directors. Directors would be required to poll the membership for investment preferences. Although these preferences would not be binding, directors would consider them in purchasing and voting stock for the fund. All investment decisions would be open to public scrutiny.

The funds would be private and competitive, licensed and closely regulated by the Securities and Exchange Commission. Managers would compete for accounts and so would be encouraged to offer the greatest return on investment commensurate with the greatest security. Since employees could remove their accounts to another fund, managers would also have an incentive to handle the money wisely and honestly.

This pension arrangement has been worked out in some detail. (See Appendix C for a more detailed summary of the plan in a speech by Ralph Nader before the Sixth Annual Conference on Employee Benefits in New York, May 24, 1972.) It offers a viable alternative to patching up the old system inadequately or abandoning private pensions completely in favor of Social Security. It would especially behoove members of the pension industry who want to keep the large sums of money contributed to pension funds in the private sector to look seriously at this kind of proposal.

There is growing interest in this proposal among members of Congress. Legislative proposals to implement such a plan are to be introduced in the Congress. Certainly this is not the only approach to overhauling the private pension system; and others should be forthcoming as the pension debate continues during the coming year.

XII

Your Turn to Play

Improvement of the private pension system cannot come about unless you and others who hope to get a pension take an active part in changing the system. There are two broad areas in which plan participants can affect their pensions: supporting private pension legislation at the national level and influencing employers and union officials to improve their plans.

It is important for you to know that no one is speaking strictly in the interests of beneficiaries to Congress or the Federal government. Certain unions are urging passage of legislation that will help plan participants. But as we have noted earlier, the interests of unions do not always coincide with those of beneficiaries. The same is even more true for employers and financial institutions that have a stake in private pensions as they exist today.

The voice of pension management is heard with far greater frequency in Washington than that of beneficiaries or anyone else on the subject of pensions. Members of the pension industry support well-organized efforts throughout the country to make their interests known. For example, the Association of Private Pension and Welfare Plans, Inc., arranges periodic meetings where industry spokesmen talk with congressmen about their views on pension legislation. The association is composed of employers, union representatives, administrators, actuaries, lawyers, bankers, and consultants. Beneficiaries are not represented.

Pension managers also belong to regional pension conferences that meet frequently with Federal officials to talk about regulation of private pension plans. They include the American Pension Conference, the Southern Pension Conference, the Midwest Pension Conference, and the Western Pension Conference. Beneficiaries are not included.

Another organization, the National Foundation of Health, Welfare and Pension Funds, sponsors conferences for trustees, administrators, actuaries, and others on the management end of private pension plans. These meetings are held in pleasant vacation spots and involve considerable cost to pension beneficiaries since trustees' attendance at the meetings is paid for from the pension funds. But beneficiaries are not invited.

In addition to these groups there are others that speak often in Washington in management's interests including the American Bankers Association, the National Association of Manufacturers and other trade groups, the U.S. Chamber of Commerce, and the large unions such as the AFL-CIO, the United Auto Workers Union, and the United Steelworkers.

What are these management groups saying to Congress? By and large, with the exception of certain unions, they are opposing regulations that would realistically protect the interests of beneficiaries. For example, Robert C. Tyson, chairman of the Finance Committee of U.S. Steel Corporation, argues that ". . . mandatory funding requirements incorporated in current legislative proposals could only lead to rigid and highly restrictive rules. . . . Bureaucratic rigidity would replace professional actuarial judgment." [1]

This is a vague argument at best. How is it to be weighed against the interests of employees in more secure benefits? How is "professional actuarial judgment" helping beneficiaries now? It is essential that employees make their views heard to make the picture complete.

The U.S. Chamber of Commerce adds its powerful voice: "The Chamber supports sound programs of funding and vesting. We oppose, however, new additional Federal minimum standards. Such standards would impose unnecessary costs on private pension plans, create a huge and costly new administrative structure, reduce flexibility in pension and related fringe-benefit planning, tend to limit free collective bargaining, and inhibit pension growth." [2]

These assertions are questionable. How helpful is "flexibility" to plan participants? Wouldn't many employees benefit from less flexibility if it meant that more of them received benefits? What are "unnecessary costs" from the point of view of beneficiaries? How are the purported "disadvantages" of minimum standards to be weighed against the loss of pension benefits by millions of workers?

The power of the Chamber of Commerce as well as its ability to block meaningful pension reform is illustrated by its legislative maneuvering that prevented a Senate vote on the Williams-Javits bill last September.

Wilbur Daniels, vice president of the International Ladies

Garment Workers Union, states that proposed vesting and funding standards "mean simply that the ILGWU retirement fund could not continue to provide the current level of modest benefits—or if the benefit levels were to be maintained, employers in the industry would be hard put to pay for the vast increase in costs which would be required." [3]

What do union members think about this? According to responses to our questionnaire, most would prefer to have reduced benefits, if necessary, in order to gain more secure benefits.

It should be noted, too, that the inevitability of "vast increases in costs" uniformly predicted by employers and unions that oppose better vesting and funding has never been proved. There is reason to believe that cost is not the overriding problem in improving pension plans that it is often purported to be. The latest such evidence came from Assistant Secretary of the Treasury Edwin S. Cohen, who told the House Ways and Means Committee on May 8, 1972, that President Nixon's vesting proposals would raise the cost of pension plans very little. The "rule of 50," Cohen said, would increase the cost of plans *at the most* by only 0.4 percent of payroll.

The Nixon proposal is, of course, extremely limited. But Assistant Secretary Cohen also assessed the added cost of the Javits-Williams bill, with somewhat more liberal vesting, as only 0.9 percent of payroll.

These cost estimates may or may not be accurate, since it is not known on what data the Treasury Department sought to defend the administration's proposals. But even if they are reasonably close, they fail to suggest the kinds of prohibitive costs generally asserted by members of the pension industry.

In all events, you should be wary when your employer or union talks to you about the "vast increases" in costs of improved plans and threatens you with reduced benefits. Ask for facts and figures and don't be satisfied with sweeping statements such as frequently meet employees' arguments for better pension plans.

The majority of pension plan participants, in contrast to management, believe that Federal regulation is essential if their interests are to be fully protected. As one employee stated: "Any type of retirement fund . . . should be fully investigated. Very few of us have either the education or the means to correct these matters [of pension fund mismanagement]. There is even the possibility of getting into trouble with the labor organizations."

A mine worker, writing of the thousands of miners denied pensions under the United Mine Workers' Welfare and Retirement Fund, spoke of the government's responsibility for protecting pension beneficiaries: "It is unbelievable that a situation which is robbing thousands of people of their pensions should continue to exist without the government taking some action. Legislation prohibiting such inhumane treatment of the working man by labor unions and industry should be introduced and passed."

Another employee pointed to the need for regulation in light of the public-supported tax subsidy granted to employers contributing to pension funds: "I think it is a darn shame that the Federal government allows some concerns to deduct the costs of the pension plan from their income taxes only to have these same concerns default in the payment of pension benefits after a few years. The Federal government approved the plan and it seems their responsibility ended right there."

Numerous people who wrote to us ended their call for improvement of private pensions with a plea for government regulation. A worker from North Kingstown, Rhode Island, said: "I would like to repeat that, although I generally do not ap-prove of the Federal government getting involved in everything, I very strongly favor Federal government standards for private pension plans."

Yet congressmen too often hear only the industry side of the question. The importance of your taking action cannot be overemphasized. No one else is speaking strictly in the interests of beneficiaries. It is up to you and the millions of other employees who expect a pension someday to take steps in your own behalf.

Thousands of disappointed pensioners have written to their congressmen seeking help in getting a pension. Letters to congressmen do have an impact. But often the impact is limited because many congressmen and senators do not understand the reasons behind the particular problems described in letters they receive. Even less do they understand the solutions for those problems. You can gain the help of your elected officials more easily if you are able to tell them clearly about the provisions of your pension plan, how they affect you, and what you think is wrong with them, *and* if you can offer solutions in terms of legislation you want them to support.

In your letters you should ask for specific responses from your congressmen or senators as to their position on the legislative proposals you support, and make it clear you will be watching their votes on the issues.

You can help your elected officials recognize the size of the pension problem if you and your fellow workers organize around issues that affect you all. You should try to arrange a meeting between your congressman and workers concerned about pensions. Most will be receptive, especially when large numbers of people are involved: organized lobbyists represent campaign contributions, but you represent votes.

Also send a copy of your letter or write directly to the Labor

Department. The letters from employees on file there have been a valuable source of information. If it had not been for these letters the dramatic story of pensions might never have been told. Write:

Leonard J. Lurie, Director
Office of Labor-Management Welfare-Pension Plan Reports
U.S. Department of Labor
8701 Georgia Avenue
Silver Spring, Maryland 20910

You may also want to seek help from the Federal government and the courts where possible. For example, if large numbers of workers are being laid off (without any pensions when they are not vested), you may want to ask the Internal Revenue Service for a ruling on whether the pension plan should be terminated. A termination ruling would give all employees a claim on the pension fund, whether or not they have nonforfeitable credits, as long as the money lasts. You can contact:

Isidore Goodman
Chief of the Pension Trust Branch
Room 6229 Internal Revenue Service
12th and Constitution Avenue, N.W.
Washington, D.C. 20220
Phone (202) 964-3871

You may also want to contact Mr. Goodman at the I.R.S. if most of the money in your pension fund is going to pay benefits to a few high-salaried employees, while most other employees are not receiving benefits. The I.R.S. has regulations against discrimination by private pension plans.

The Internal Revenue Service and the Labor Department

are authorized to issue regulations to enforce the tax and disclosure laws related to pensions. If you believe that these agencies are not fulfilling their regulatory duties, you can file a petition asking that they take specific action. Last year we filed a petition with the Labor Department asking the agency to exercise its authority to require more meaningful disclosure of information to pension plan participants. In our petition we suggested that the disclosure requirements were not adequately met when employers simply gave copies of the plan to employees. Many employees understandably fail to interpret the complicated legal language; full communication means simple and direct statements. We also argued that full disclosure should include telling employees when they might *not* get a benefit under the pension plan, as well as when they will. The Labor Department has subsequently proposed additional disclosure requirements. (See Appendix E for Ralph Nader's petition for more meaningful communication with plan participants and the Labor Department's proposed new rules.)

Other government agencies may also be involved with private pensions. For example, some of the money paid by the Department of Defense for defense procurement goes to support pensions for workers in the defense industry. However, thousands of these workers are not getting pension benefits because of frequent layoffs. Recently, several engineers petitioned the Defense Department to make sure that the workers for whom contributions are made actually receive pensions. The petition was denied; however, it raised the question of the government's responsibility in this area and pointed to a need for action. Senator Javits has now proposed an amendment to a pending bill, S. 32, that would make explicit the government's responsibility to protect scientists and engineers from pension forfeitures by making the protection of benefit rights a condition of compliance with Federal procurement regulations. (See Appendix D for the petition to the Department of Defense.)

If you suspect your pension fund money is being used illegally, for example to benefit fund trustees or their friends, contact:

>Charles Ruff
>Management and Labor Section,
>   Criminal Division
>U.S. Department of Justice, Room 1333
>Washington, D.C. 20530

>or

>Ed Daly, Chief Investigator
>Office of Labor-Management
>   Welfare—Pension Plan Reports
>U.S. Department of Labor
>8701 Georgia Avenue
>Silver Spring, Maryland 20910

If Federal officials tell you that they cannot act in your behalf, you may want to bring a court suit. Court action can be expensive, of course, but it is one alternative. You may have evidence that your fund monies are being abused by the trustees, in which case you need legal advice and representation. Or an individual employee may believe he has been denied his pension unjustly; his case may be used to challenge the administration of the fund in general as "arbitrary and capricious." An employee may challenge the action of plan trustees through an appeals procedure, if any (there almost never is provision for appeal). If he is represented by a union, he may ask the union to help him process a grievance. If the union refuses, as has occasionally happened in pension cases, he may want to seek advice on the union's action from his regional office of the National Labor Relations Board. To locate the regional office, write:

>NLRB
>1717 Pennsylvania Avenue, N.W.
>Washington, D.C. 20570

Finally, he may want to contact a lawyer.

Some lawyers may take your case on a *"pro bono"* basis (as a public service) or for a reduced fee. Sometimes courts have awarded lawyers fees in cases involving disappointed pensioners. That was the case, for example, with the mine workers who sued the trustees of their retirement fund and were represented by lawyers *pro bono*. The number of lawyers and law firms offering this kind of assistance is growing but still limited. How do you find a lawyer?

First call your local bar association's referral service and ask for the names of lawyers who do public interest work. Don't be disappointed if the bar association can't help you; but it is worth a try. The next place to look is the local legal services office. Most communities have a lawyer or group of lawyers, usually working under a government grant, who provide legal services for people who can't afford the expenses of litigation. These lawyers may be listed under various titles, such as legal aid society, legal services, or neighborhood legal services. The local bar association can probably direct you to them or you may find them in your telephone book. (If you have trouble locating a legal services office, write to Office of Legal Services, U.S. Office of Economic Opportunity, Washington, D.C.)

The legal aid lawyer may not be able to represent you himself: your income must be below a certain level for him to help you. However, he can probably give you the names of lawyers in your community who are interested in doing *pro bono* work. Or he may tell you of lawyers who might take your case on a "contingent fee" basis. This means that the lawyer will get a percentage of whatever you collect—or nothing if you lose the case. Lawyers might be especially interested in taking a case on a contingent fee basis if a group of employees were involved or if a case were filed for a "class" of citizens, namely all employees affected by certain pension practices, since recovery would be larger.

The U.S. Office of Economic Opportunity also funds legal offices that provide back-up assistance to local attorneys in certain areas such as pensions. These offices could be helpful since most lawyers are not familiar with legal problems in the pension area and those who are generally represent employers only. You or your lawyer may want to contact:

> The National Senior Citizens Law Center
> 1709 West Eighth Street, Suite 600
> Los Angeles, California 90017
>
> or
>
> The National Senior Citizens Law Center
> 1511 K Street, N.W.
> Washington, D.C. 20005

Pension plan participants are often indignant over their powerlessness in influencing management of their plans. Most people who wrote to us agreed with the employee who said: "Private pensions should have some provisions for an employee beneficiary to have some voice in its management and distribution, especially since he accepts an equity in lieu of salary during his employment."

In some instances, you can take effective action to change your plan in your company or union. The first step is to gain information.

The right to know

The law gives you the right to a written statement describing your pension plan if you request it. If you are refused, you can file suit to enforce your right. Also, a plan description must always be on hand at the head office of the employer or plan administrator. In addition, the Labor Department has a copy of the plan description on file.

New regulations expanding your right to know have been proposed by the Labor Department, as we mentioned earlier. They include the requirement that employees must be notified in writing of their right to receive plan descriptions and copies of the plan's annual reports. The new regulations will also require that plan descriptions be written in simple language that is easy for laymen to understand. (Administrators often simply give employees copies of the plan itself written in legal jargon difficult for anyone to interpret.)

Also, under the new proposed regulations, you must be told of circumstances under which you might *not* receive your pension. (See Appendix E.)

If you have any trouble getting these documents, write to:

> W. J. Usery, Assistant Secretary of Labor
> Labor Management Services Administration
> Room 3137, Department of Labor
> 14th and Constitution Avenue, N.W.
> Washington, D.C. 20210

Meetings with pension officials

You should also insist on meeting with pension plan officials for detailed explanations of the plan. These meetings can take place when the company first presents the plan to employees or when the union holds a meeting so that members can vote to ratify the plan. (Don't vote for ratification until *all* your questions are answered to your satisfaction.) If your plan is already in effect, request a meeting with your company personnel officer or with union representatives. Remember, you have a right to know.

What you want to know about your pension

In the preceding chapters we have outlined certain questions you may want to ask about your pension plan. Refer to the last few pages of each chapter for suggested questions and courses of action with regard to vesting conditions (Chapter V), possibilities for losing your pension (Chapter VI), funding (Chapter VII), administration (Chapters VIII and IX), survivors' benefits (Chapter X). The following is a brief review of the kinds of information you need:

1. What will you get from the pension plan: (a) if you quit your job today; (b) if you work under the plan until retirement?
2. How is the size of your benefit determined? Is it a fixed benefit? Does it depend on the number of years worked? On years worked and salary over your entire career? On your salary in the years of highest pay or during the last five or ten years of employment?
3. What might cause you to lose your pension: (a) if you

leave the company; (b) if you change unions or union locals; (c) if you are laid off for a certain period of time?

4. Will your years worked before the plan was established count toward a pension?
5. How many people currently employed under the plan are expected to receive a pension?
6. If you are under a multiemployer plan, what companies and unions are part of the plan?
7. Under any kind of plan are there reciprocity agreements that will allow you to change jobs and carry your credits with you? If so, what industries and unions are involved and where are they located?
8. Does your plan offer a survivor's benefit? Is it optional, and if so, how do you go about choosing a survivor's benefit? Does the employer contribute anything to help pay for the survivor's benefit?
9. Does your plan include cost-of-living provisions? Does it offer "equity annuity" provisions allowing you to gear part of the contributions made on your behalf to the stock market?
10. How do you apply for a pension: (a) if you retire while still working under the plan; (b) if you leave the company before you retire?
11. What are the conditions for keeping a pension after you have retired?
12. What would happen if your plan terminated today? Will there be enough money for everyone? Will benefits be paid only to those with nonforfeitable benefit rights? Will they be paid only to employees who are already retired or over age sixty? If there is not enough money for everyone, what will you get?
13. Does your employer make regular contributions to the pension fund or does he pay benefits as qualified workers

retire? If he makes contributions, are they specified, for example, by a union contract? Have the contributions increased or decreased recently?
14. If the employer makes regular contributions, do the contributions cover credits earned *before* the plan was set up?
15. At what date will the plan have enough money on hand to cover all credits?
16. Who administers your plan? That is, who decides which employees qualify for benefits and authorizes payments of benefits? (This is usually a pension board, which may be comprised of corporate officers or of management and union officials. Sometimes third-party representatives are appointed to the pension board.)
17. Who takes care of the money? That is, who is legally responsible as fund trustee for management of the funds that are supposed to pay you a benefit? A bank? An insurance company? Several financial institutions, such as banks, insurance companies, and investment firms?
18. Does the employer or pension board have any control over investment of the funds by the trustee?
19. Where are funds invested? How do trustees exercise their proxy voting power? Do they consult beneficiaries in making investments or voting decisions?
20. What is the rate of earnings?
21. How much money is going into administration of the plan?

Organizing to change the plan

Many of your plan provisions may not satisfy you. Certainly you should be very concerned if your plan requires you to work until retirement before you gain nonforfeitable rights to a benefit. Your priority may then be the inclusion of vesting provisions.

If you are in an industry with high job turnover, you may have reason for concern even if your plan grants comparatively "liberal" vesting conditions. One case might be a low-wage industry where business is declining and large numbers of workers are losing jobs. Under these conditions you will want to encourage not only early vesting but also reciprocity agreements with other industries or unions on a nationwide basis to allow you to change jobs without forfeiting pension credits.

You may find that your pension fund monies are invested in ways you don't like. Perhaps they are invested in a company that is a notorious polluter, and you would prefer to see your money put somewhere else. You may want your monies to be invested in areas that will indirectly benefit you, for example in low-cost housing.

Or survivors' benefits may be—and in many plans should be—a most important issue to work for.

Use this book to help you analyze your plan and identify those areas where improvements are needed. You may do this alone, but it would be helpful if you and several fellow employees make a joint analysis and come up with one or two issues that you want to tackle first. You will want to consider, of course, issues that will be most important to *all* employees, because without their support you will get nowhere. However, before soliciting the opinions and aid of the rest of the company's labor force, it will be helpful to clarify issues in a "core group."

1. Your first action* is to call a meeting of employees to discuss the pension plan. Some basic steps are necessary for any meeting of this kind to be a success. First, schedule a

---

* More details on citizen organizing for action will be made available in a public citizen action manual by Donald Ross, to be published in 1973.

convenient meeting place. Next, decide how to tell workers about the meeting.

Posters. Check to see whether they are allowed in the plant or office building. You may want to use bulletin boards in churches or local civic clubs. Use large lettering to get across basic information about the meeting (when, where, what it's about, etc.).

Mimeograph sheets on the purpose of the meeting. These should also be brief and designed to attract attention. If your concern is vesting, you might begin with the following: "You can work 20 years and lose your pension under the ——— Company Retirement Plan. People are losing out. You may lose out. Come discuss Your Pension Plan. . . ." If these sheets cannot be handed out inside the building, stand at entrances or find other ways to make sure all employees receive them.

Personal contacts. Personally solicit people to come to the meeting. Attendance cannot be left to chance. The core group may want to recruit others to help telephone as many employees as possible to tell them in person about the meeting.

2. *The Meeting.* Plan the meeting carefully so that it doesn't disintegrate into a free-for-all discussion with nothing accomplished. Choose a moderator and draw up an agenda in advance. *Be sure you know what you want to come out of the meeting*—a petition, a vote on certain issues, a vote on sending a group to meet with the employer, union, or congressman, etc.

You may want to begin with a brief statement about the provision or provisions in the pension plan that concern you. It is effective to have several employees or former employees relate how they lost their benefits under the plan.

Or widows of employees without survivors benefits may talk about what it means to live on Social Security alone.

Next explain clearly and briefly your ideas (or the core group's ideas) about the need for reform.

Make your proposals for action and open the meeting for questions and debate.

Be sure to get the names, addresses, and phone numbers of everyone at the meeting. If another meeting is scheduled, announce it on the spot and ask everyone to bring one or two friends.

3. *Proposals for action.* The most direct approach, of course, is to go to your employer or union to discuss changes in the plan. Have clear evidence of support for these changes from as many fellow employees as possible. A petition is tangible proof of support. Or you may want to invite your employer or his representative to a meeting with interested employees. (If this is your course, do everything possible to alert employees to the meeting. Be sure to organize it well, with one or two appointed spokesmen, so that you can ask concrete questions and get answers to them.)

Suppose your employer turns a deaf ear to your proposals. At this point, or even before, you need to build support for improving the pension plan not only within the ranks of employees, but also in the community.

Use flesh-and-blood examples to get your message across to others. The local newspaper may want to interview an employee who lost his pension after twenty years with the company (or another case) and publish a story on the pension plan. A local radio commentator may do the same. Letters to the editor of the newspaper may help create interest in your problem.

In addition to public appeals for help, personally contact community leaders who may intervene with your employer. Ministers are one example.

Contact groups in the area to work with you. Organizations for retired people and senior citizens' groups are interested in the issue of retirement income and are your natural allies. For a list of such groups in your area write:

> National Council of Senior Citizens
> 1511 K Street, N.W.
> Washington, D.C. 20005

In some cases, your most diligent efforts to find out how the pension plan is managed will not succeed. Neither, in certain instances, will your efforts to improve the plan. That is why broader disclosure requirements and regulation of pension funds by law are important. Employees cannot be solely responsible for monitoring their pension fund or seeing that plans are managed in their best interests. Better fiduciary and disclosure laws, if passed, will provide protection in areas where you may not be able to protect yourself. So will requirements for earlier vesting, funding standards, and plan insurance. But your participation is essential in order that the kinds of legislation that may be passed reflect employees' interests and not just the interests of those who manage private pension plans.

Appendices

APPENDIX A

Pension Questionnaire

The following questionnaire was mailed with a covering letter and pension fact sheet to 839 people who had written about pensions to us, to the Senate Labor Subcommittee, the House General Labor Subcommittee, and to the Labor Department. Of those mailed 537 were returned completed; eighty-one were returned unopened.

More than half the respondents were receiving or expected to receive a private pension benefit. Slightly fewer than one-half were retired; one-third were over sixty-five. One-fourth were female. Answers came from forty states.

Remarks on the questionnaires indicated that two questions were construed in different ways so that their answers are not clearcut. On question 4, some people indicated they were thinking of why companies *do* offer pensions, such as union pressure, while most respondents gave reasons they thought companies *should* provide them (as was intended). The intent of question 7-1 was to determine employees' preference for a minimum age requirement for vesting. However, most people appeared to answer according to their own experience with vesting rather than their preference. For example, a respondent who gave twenty years service as a vesting requirement noted that he had worked twenty-one years but was not yet vested under his plan. This employee thought that he should have vested rights by this time. The same was true for others who seemed to be answering on the basis of having worked twenty or twenty-five years without acquiring vested benefit rights.

Since respondents sometimes omitted answering one or two questions, totals do not always come to the full 537.

1. City _____ State _____
   Age: under 55, *182* / 55–64, *171* / over 65, *173*
   Sex: M, *415* / F, *115*   Retired? yes *233* / no *294*
2. Do you receive (or expect to receive) benefits from a private pension plan? yes *293* no *214*
3. If you were to describe the money that companies put into a pension fund, would you say the money is more like
   (a) *gifts* to employees? *114* or
   (b) *wages* earned by employees? *405*
4. Why should companies provide pension benefits?
   (a) so that retired employees will have enough money to live on? *300* or
   (b) so that employees will want to stay with a company until retirement? *86* or
   (c) other? *112: The most common answers were tax incentives and union pressure.*
5. If you had to choose, would you rather see
   (a) higher social security retirement benefits for everybody? *236* or
   (b) more people getting private pension benefits? *245*
6. If you could change the private pension system in only one way, would you provide
   (a) more money for persons now getting private pension benefits? *148* or
   (b) private pension benefits for more people? *305*
7. Do you think that a company should pay pension benefits at retirement to employees who leave that company before retirement? yes *462* no *69*
   7.1 If your answer is yes, how many years should an employee be required to work for a company in order to receive at retirement 100% of the pension benefits based upon his period of employment with that company? 25? *76* 20? *146* 15? *61* 10? *66* 5? *36* 3? *13* 1? *22* other? *40*

7.2 Should there be a requirement that the employee also have reached a specified age at the time he leaves the company? yes *179* no *269* If yes, what age? under 55: *52*; 55–64: *98*; over 65: *29*.

7.3 If your answer to #7 is yes, would your answer be the same if the company contributed a smaller amount of money to the pension fund for each employee each year than it would have contributed if benefits were paid only to employees working for the company at the time they retired? yes *252* no *100*

7.4 If your answer to #7 is yes, should the company paying the pension benefits
   (a) hold on to the benefits until the employee retires? *30* or
   (b) transfer the employee's benefits to his employer? *18* or
   (c) transfer the employee's benefits to a retirement account in his name administered by a bank or an insurance company? *124* or
   (d) transfer the employee's benefits to a retirement account in his name in a fund administered by the Federal government? *164* or
   (e) other? *48 (25 of these marked c and d)*

8. (a) Should pension funds be insured so that if companies go out of business or for some other reason there is not enough money in a pension fund, the promised benefits will be paid? yes *514* no *12*
   (b) Should pension plans provide for benefits for the dependent widows and widowers of retired employees? yes *479* no *38*
   If your answers to (a) and/or (b) are yes, would your answers be the same if it was necessary to reduce employee benefits to cover added costs?
   8(a) yes *352* no *110;* 8(b) yes *298* no *91*

9. Should employees who may benefit from a fund have any say in (a) who administers the pension fund and/or (b) the type of investments made by the fund?
   9(a) yes *455* no *45;* 9(b) yes *342* no *83*

10. Do you think that more people would put more money aside for their retirement if they did not have to pay taxes on that money? yes *400* no *114*

If you have comments or questions, please write them on the back of this questionnaire.

YOU AND YOUR PENSION

Dear Friend:

I am writing to you because you have firsthand knowledge about pensions and may wish to express your views on issues of pension reform.

The Office of Labor-Management and Welfare-Pension Reports of the U.S. Department of Labor made your name and address available to my office pursuant to a formal request—along with the names of 1000 other persons who have written to the Federal government about pensions—in order to make it possible for you to communicate your opinions on pension issues to members of Congress.

Congress is and will be considering a number of proposals for changes in the private pension system. The persons who are being heard in support of and opposition to these proposals are persons who will not be affected by the system. Their retirement income is secure and ample. Your voice should also be heard.

The enclosed questionnaire sets forth several of the pension issues. These issues are not easy either to communicate or to decide; nevertheless, they must be decided by Congress. They should be decided with your help.

For your convenience and the convenience of Congress, you may want to return the completed questionnaire to my office. Your answers will be summarized along with those of hundreds of others in a Pension Report which I shall deliver to each member of Congress.

I sincerely hope that you will take the time to join in this project. Your participation may make old age less uncomfortable for millions of Americans.

Yours very truly,

/s/ Ralph Nader

Enc.

Pension Fact Sheet

More than one-half the private work force does not work for a company or union that has a pension plan.

At least one-half of all persons participating in private pension plans may not receive pension benefits when they retire.

More than one-half of all persons who will receive private pension benefits will receive less than $1000 a year.

Many pension plans do not provide for benefits for dependent widows or widowers, or provide very limited benefits.

Pension fund administrators have been known to make unwise investments and even to appropriate pension money for their own use.

Some administrators control such large amounts of money that they can control corporations and affect the stock market.

APPENDIX B

Pending Pension Legislation

To express your opinion of pension legislation or to get copies of particular bills, write to the sponsor of a bill and to the chairman of the committee to which the bill is referred. All congressmen may be reached by writing The Capitol, Washington, D.C., or telephoning (202) 224-3121. Specific addresses are given for sponsors of major pension legislation.

The major bills relating to private pensions are the following (numbers are as introduced in the 92nd Congress):

S. 3598.   Introduced by Senator Harrison A. Williams, Jr., D-N.J., (Old Senate Office Building, Room 352, (202) 225-4744) and Senator Jacob Javits, R-N.Y. (Old Senate Office Building, Room 320, (202) 225-6542)

This bill is discussed in Chapter XI. Referred to Senate Committee on Labor and Public Welfare, Senator Williams, Chairman.

S. 2.   Introduced by Senator Javits.

Replaced by the Williams-Javits compromise bill. (S. 2 was stronger in that it provided for a central pension commission

APPENDIX B

to consolidate all regulation of private pension plans.) See Chapter XI.

Referred to Senate Committee on Labor and Public Welfare.

S. 3012. Introduced by Senator Carl T. Curtis, R-Neb. (New Senate Office Building, Room 5311, (202) 225-4224)

The Nixon administration bill on vesting, tax deductions for personal retirement savings, and increased limits on pension contributions by the self-employed. See Chapter XI.

Referred to Senate Committee on Finance, Senator Russell Long, Chairman.

S. 3024. Introduced by Senator Javits.

The Nixon administration fiduciary proposals. See Chapter XI.

Referred to Senate Committee on Labor and Public Welfare.

S. 2485. Introduced by Senator Robert P. Griffin, R-Mich. (Old Senate Office Building, Room 353, (202) 225-6221)

To provide a wholly owned government corporation in the Treasury Department to operate a pension plan reinsurance program; to provide vesting requirements of 100 percent vesting after fifteen years cumulative service initially; eventually to provide 100 percent vesting after ten years employment; to cover plans with more than fifteen participants; to direct the Secretary of the Treasury to study portability.

Referred to the Senate Committee on Finance.

S. 2486. Introduced by Senator Griffin.

To amend the Welfare and Pension Plans Disclosure Act to strengthen fiduciary and disclosure requirements.

Referred to Senate Committee on Labor and Public Welfare.

S. 1993. Introduced by Senator Vance Hartke, D-Ind. (Old Senate Office Building, Room 451, (202) 225-4814)

To establish a self-supporting pension plan reinsurance program in the Labor Department.

Referred to the Senate Committee on Finance.

H.R. 1269. Introduced by Rep. John Dent, D-Pa. (Rayburn House Office Building, Room 2430, (202) 225-5631)

This bill is discussed in Chapter XI.

Referred to House Committee on Education and Labor, General Labor Subcommittee, Rep. Dent, Chairman.

H.R. 14982. Introduced by Rep. Peter W. Rodino, D-N.J.

Same as S. 3598.

Referred to House Ways and Means Committee, Rep. Wilbur Mills, Chairman.

H.R. 12337. Introduced by Rep. John N. Erlenborn, R-Ill. (Cannon House Office Building, Room 330, (202) 225-3515)

The Nixon administration proposals to provide for fiduciary and disclosure standards. Same as S. 3024.

Referred to House Committee on Education and Labor.

H.R. 12272. Introduced by Rep. Wilbur Mills, D-Ark., by request. (Longworth House Office Building, Room 1136, (202) 225-2506)

The Nixon proposals for vesting, individual savings, and contributions to pensions by the self-employed. Same as S. 3012.

Referred to the House Ways and Means Committee.

The following bills are more limited or are similar to major proposals listed above. You may want to write for copies of the bills and to ask their sponsors what they are doing in support of them in order to determine how serious they are about pension reform.

H.R. 12124. Introduced by Rep. Peter A. Peyser, R-N.Y. (Longworth House Office Building, Room 1133, (202) 225-5536)

To require optional annuities for surviving spouses in private

APPENDIX B

pension plans and certain vesting rights for employees whose employment is involuntarily terminated.

Referred to House Committee on Education and Labor.

H.R. 3823. Introduced by Rep. Henry Helstoski, D-N.J.

Same as S. 2.

Referred to House Ways and Means Committee.

H.R. 6122. Introduced by Rep. Charles J. Carney, D-Ohio.

Same as S. 2 in vesting, funding, and portability provisions; similar to H.R. 1269 in fiduciary provisions.

Referred to House Ways and Means Committee.

H.R. 686. Introduced by Rep. John Dingell, D-Mich.

Similar to S. 2; provides for a voluntary portability program administered by the Department of Health, Education and Welfare, amending the Social Security Act. Provides for full vesting in ten years.

Referred to House Ways and Means Committee.

H.R. 2150. Introduced by Rep. Harold R. Collier, R-Ill.

Similar to H.R. 1269 except for more extensive exemptions from funding requirements.

Referred to House Committee on Education and Labor.

H.R. 6530. Introduced by Rep. Seymour Halpern, D-N.Y.

Similar to S. 2 except for variations on funding vesting standards.

Referred to House Ways and Means Committee.

APPENDIX C

Remarks by Ralph Nader before the Sixth Annual
Conference on Employee Benefits,
New York City, May 24, 1972

In terms of dollar impact, the private pension system represents one of the most comprehensive consumer frauds that many Americans will encounter in their lifetime. And I use the term "fraud" advisedly.

Those of you who sell, service, and administer private pension plans, as well as those who negotiate and establish plans, have seriously and deliberately misrepresented the nature of this pension system. The industry has induced some 30 million Americans to rely on the system's promise of retirement security knowing full well that the system can afford to provide that security to very few. At least one-half of all persons participating in private pension plans will not receive pension benefits when they retire. More than one-half of all persons who receive private pension benefits receive less than $1000 a year. The majority of pension plans do not provide for benefits for dependent widows or widowers, or provide very limited benefits. This vast 151 billion dollar system—heavily subsidized by an annual Federal tax subsidy of well over 3 billion dollars a year—is hurting too many people unnecessarily and unfairly.

The problem is not, as many of you like to contend, simply a problem of communication. It is a problem which goes to the very essence of the system.

The response of many of you to the petition I filed with the Secretary of Labor last July made that all too clear.

In that petition I asked the Secretary to exercise his authority under the Welfare and Pension Plans Disclosure Act to require plan administrators to advise plan participants in negative and unambiguous language of circumstances under which they or their survivors might not or would not receive pension benefits. Your immediate reaction was that this would be disastrous. If employees were made aware of the contingent nature of their promised benefits, they might not want pension plans!

Although you quickly withdrew this objection, it had its effect. The rule proposed by the Department of Labor on February 1st of this year, while acknowledging that plan administrators do have an obligation to advise participants of the circumstances under which they may not receive benefits, would allow administrators to satisfy this obligation in such a way that only the most diligent of employees would ever be likely to discover the limitations of their plans. The rule would also ensure that those few employees who do manage to read these provisions could rely on them only at their peril. It would be difficult to find a better expression of what appears to be the prevailing industry ethic: the less employees know about the operation of the pension system, the better.

What is disconcerting is to find this attitude emerge from the Department of Labor, the government agency generally considered to be the advocate for the interests of employees. [The explanation may be that the department acted on the recommendation of its Advisory Council on Employee Welfare and Pension Benefit Plans, which has a minimum of ten of its thirteen members with strong "vested" interests in the present operation of the pension system and no members specifically representing the interests of the millions of persons who have been or will be hurt by the pension system.]

If the promises of the pension system have been seriously misrepresented, so have the promises of reform legislation. Certainly, you are aware of the deficiencies of the reform bills now pending in Congress, but most of the rest of the American public is not.

When President Nixon summarized the administration pension bill to the White House Conference on Aging, how many of the thousands of assembled delegates understood the potential impact of that bill on their daily lives? The President's bill is specifically supposed to help the older worker. But how many older workers have been made aware that enactment of the bill might cost them their jobs or make it even more difficult than it now is for them to find new jobs with pension coverage? How many of their wives appreciate the fact that their already limited chance of receiving survivors' benefits might be diminished even further, since survivors' benefit provisions are often the first to go in a cost squeeze? And were retirees now receiving pensions told that their former employers would be even less apt to raise the levels of their already inadequate benefits? Of course not. Yet these are all facts material to a fair assessment of the bill, as are the even more critical fact that vesting provisions without funding standards can only create even more disappointed expectations, and the fact that few employees will be able to take advantage of tax deferral provisions permitting them to save for their own retirement.

Senators Williams and Javits have also not been entirely candid about the scope of their bill. Although the senators have done an excellent job in detailing the many problems of the pension system, their solution is by no means as "comprehensive" as they would like it to appear. Senator Javits has characterized the administration bill as a "Band-aid" approach, but is the new Williams-Javits bill more than a more elaborate patching-up effort?

What does the bill do for the engineer who in a forty year work history will never work more than six years for one employer? Or for the sales clerk who will work continuously for an employer who can't afford the administrative costs involved in setting up a pension plan? Or the auto mechanic whose plan is under a forty year funding schedule, but the plan terminates after five years? Or the insurance executive fired before his eighth year, the garment worker whose plan will be granted a variance, or the housewife who will receive nothing if her husband predeceases her? The bill does nothing for these persons, and it does very little even for those employees who may be luckier. The employee who works for eight years for a company gets something, 30 percent or 2.4 years' worth of a pension, but frozen at its value when he leaves the company. That isn't much, and he may not be able to pick up too much more in bits and pieces from other employers, particularly as after each job change he must satisfy new eligibility requirements.

The bill's sponsors concede in private that it is not adequate, but argue that it's a first step in the direction of meaningful reform. As many of you know, I take issue with that assumption. I seriously doubt that once the loudest and most outraged cries have been silenced, there will ever again be enough public pressure for a second step. But regardless, it is certainly incumbent upon all sponsors of pension legislation to disclose to their constituents all facts material to a full and fair consideration of the nature and extent of the reform proposed.

The ultimate responsibility for the misrepresentation of proposed pension reform legislation is not to be found in the administration or Congress. The responsibility is yours. The pension industry has made it clear that its phenomenal economic and political power will be used to ensure that there is as little meaningful reform as possible. Your efforts to forestall the enactment of truly comprehensive legislation represent a classic case study of the influence of special interests on our legislative processes.

Not only do you have members of the U.S. Chamber of Commerce, the National Association of Manufacturers, the American Bankers Association, and the Life Insurance Association of America in almost continual communication with members of Congress and the administration, you also have the Association of Private Pension and Welfare Plans, Inc., a main purpose of which is to arrange meetings for industry representatives with senators and congressmen, and the ad hoc groups from the several regional pension conferences which make it their business to call repeatedly on every person in Washington who might conceivably be in a policy-making position. Some of you neglect nothing including encouraging key congressional staffers to adopt legislative proposals you know to be politically unfeasible, solely as a means of distracting attention from more viable alternatives. Others guarantee that a professional association will report out position papers favorable to your interests by making sure that its members know that their statements will be relayed back to their clients. Still others put forward studies that you know are based on unrepresentative samples. And all of this has considerable effect: bills are introduced which are increasingly less comprehensive, more "acceptable" to that curious pension coalition of industry and organized labor.

None of this would be particularly remarkable but for the fact that no one is being heard on the other side. Compromises are being made, not of opposing views, but all from the same starting point—do as little as possible. No one is representing the interests of persons hurt by the system; the usual adversary process isn't operative. [It is also not working, I might add, in the courts. Despite a few significant breakthroughs, it is still virtually impossible for employees to get representation in pension cases, even if they can afford to pay. A member of my staff tried to find a lawyer for a pension claimant here in New York and learned that most pension lawyers consider themselves employer lawyers and will not represent employees, even where there is no possibility of a conflict of interest. Last year at another pension industry conference I suggested that you undertake to establish a clearinghouse for pension complaints. In response to the suggestion I was contacted by several lawyers and actuaries around the country willing to volunteer their services. All that is now needed is minimal funding by your industry, and a small administrative staff.]

In the absence of representation of the interests of beneficiaries before Congress, the intensity of industry lobbying seems somewhat strange. It is particularly so, given the fact that sole reason for the existence of the industry is to ensure the well-being of the persons whose interests you so actively oppose. Many of you are fiduciaries, obligated by law to act in the best interests of pension beneficiaries. Even if you do not actively support realistic reform legislation, as I think your fiduciary responsibility requires you to, at the very least it is incumbent upon you not to oppose it.

The financial community has consistently taken an unduly narrow view of fiduciary responsibility. Even though you acknowledge that you have a responsibility to seek a maximum return (consistent with safety) on pension money, you have not acted effectively to rid yourselves of the interlocking directorates and other conflicting interests that may adversely affect pension fund performance.

Even more important, you have failed to recognize that pension beneficiaries are a unique class of beneficiaries and that their money is allocated to a very special use—providing income at retirement. From this perspective yield, although important (particularly when increased earnings are used to increase benefits), is not the only consideration in determining the best interests of beneficiaries. High benefits are meaningless to a retiree who faces even higher costs at retirement. His concern is with his *real* income—his income less expenses. A higher benefit is of no use to him if he cannot afford a place to live because there is a housing shortage. It won't help him if he must pay large amounts for medical care because he has been maimed in an unsafe factory or automobile or has emphysema aggravated by polluted air. And his interests will have been substantially disserved if he can't afford to purchase essential consumer goods because his pension money has been invested to increase concentration and decrease competition among the manufacturers of those goods. I submit that for these reasons such considerations may be very relevant to your investment of pension fund money. Is it too much to expect you to take longer run concerns into account in addition to maintaining shorter run concerns? Consider what has happened to societies in the past who chose myopia?

Partly in response to the concern of a number of trust officers and insurance company administrators who expressed a genuine interest in responsible investment of pension fund monies but who were unclear as to what mechanism to use to ascertain the interests of those beneficiaries, I put forward a suggestion last year for a possible restructuring of the pension system to achieve that end. The idea, which was later published in the September issue of "Pension and Welfare News" met with widespread interest within the industry and considerable enthusiasm by members of Congress. The suggestion was a means of preserving capital in the private sector, while at the same time providing an equitable means of guaranteeing retirement security.

To summarize, I proposed the creation of a limited number of private, competitive, cooperative, insured institutions to be licensed and regulated by the Securities and Exchange Commission. These institutions would be empowered to receive contributions made by employers for their employees and by employees and self-employed persons for themselves and their defendent spouses. All contributions to these institutions would be tax deductible and the funds' earnings would be exempt from taxation.

Employees and self-employed persons would choose the institution where their contributions would be invested. Each person could belong to only one such institution at a time, although he could transfer his money to another fund if dissatisfied with the investment or other practices of his original fund.

An individual's contributions would be pooled for investment purposes with all other employee contributions and a pro rata share of the fund's earnings each year would be credited to his account. Each employee would have a passbook indicating the total amount in his account. At any time that he opted to file a declaration of retirement (but only one time during his life), he would begin receiving a lifetime annuity calculated on the basis of the total amount in his account and his actuarily determined life expectancy. He would also receive a cost of living adjustment to the extent of amounts available to the fund.

The directors of each fund would be representative of the fund membership and would also include persons with appropriate financial expertise. They would be subject to reelection by fund members, much as corporate officers are elected, and officers would be appointed by the directors.

The fund charters would outline the fiduciary responsibility of fund officers and directors and would specifically provide for prudent socially responsible investments. The directors would seek guidance in making investment decisions by sending investment and proxy voting preference questionnaires to fund participants. The questionnaires would not be binding on the directors. All investment decision would be open to public scrutiny.

This proposal has now been worked out in its details but the basic outline remains the same.

Three questions were raised by industry members about the proposal: would there be enough money available to a fund participant when he retired?; how could the proposed system be instituted without hurting those persons who expect to benefit from the present system?; and finally, what about increases in the cost of living? Let the following tentative thoughts serve as discussion-starters:

First, would there be enough money? Those of you who are actuaries know that there would be. An oversimplified and extremely conservative example will illustrate. The average American worker earns roughly $9000 a year. Assume that his earnings remain constant over his lifetime and that he works from age twenty-five to age sixty-five. Assume also that his employer puts an amount equal to 4 percent of the employee's pay into the employee's pension account and that this money earns 3 percent a year. Given a life expectancy of fifteen years at retirement, that employee could count on a pension benefit of roughly $2200 a year, considerably more than the current average private pension benefit, which is estimated to be less than $1000 a year.

The second question dealt with the problem of a transition to the new system. How could the proposed system be instituted without hurting those under present plans, particularly the older workers. What about making explicit what is implicit in the present system? Why not use the money theoretically allocable to younger employees to pay the benefits of older employees?

Let me be more specific. Employees assume that a certain percentage of their pay is being withheld in order to pay for their pension benefits. In fact, ordinarily pension contributions are determined in terms of percentage of payroll not percentage of pay, and the amounts paid into the pension fund are used to pay the benefits of retirees and older workers, particularly those with past service credits.

What I suggest is that for purposes of the transition employers should first calculate their pension contributions in terms of a percentage of each employee's pay and then pay these contributions as follows: (1) all contributions allocable to employees now covered by the existing pension plan to the fund established by that plan; (2) all contributions allocable to new employees who are thirty-five years or older to their accounts in one of the new pension institutions; (3) all contributions allocable to new employees who are under thirty-five years to the pension fund established under the old plan. I have been told that this would make it possible for all employees now covered by pension plans to receive the benefits they have been promised by those plans. In addition all new employees would be guaranteed at least some coverage—up to thirty years of coverage for the younger employees—under the new system. In time, perhaps in ten years, the age thirty-five cut-off date could be reduced to age thirty—or earlier if a fund is able to pay all previously promised benefits before then. In another ten years the age cut-off could be reduced to age twenty-five or three years of service, whichever is less. At that time the transition would be complete and all participants would be able to contribute to the new system for at least forty years.

(During the transition period it would also be possible for employees and self-employed persons to contribute to their own retirement fund accounts, and for employers, if they chose to do so, to transfer employees' discounted vested pension rights to these accounts. In addition it would be open to employers to terminate existing plans and distribute the money to individual accounts in accordance with the plan's termination schedule. Such a distribution might also take place in three-fourths of the employees covered by a given plan voted for termination.)

Under this approach all benefits that have been promised by existing plans would be paid. Participants would receive no less than they now can expect to receive. They also would receive no more. Those who are now programmed to lose out because of unrealistic vesting or funding requirements would still lose out. (Unless, of course, the employer is in a position to accelerate the transition. If so, he could then improve vesting provisions and funding and even increase benefit levels.)

The answer for those persons already scheduled to lose the pension "lottery," and particularly for those who have already lost, is not to apply first-aid to the system but to provide a direct and immediately effective retired workers' subsidy. This might be an amount which, added to income from all other sources, would ensure that every American over sixty-five years of age would be able to live at least at the poverty level (and preferably at the low-income level). It is incredible that one-fourth of our aged population is now forced to live below the poverty level. This subsidy would be a temporary measure, phasing itself out as the public and private retirement systems begin to live up to their promises of a decent retirement for all. The money for the subsidy could come from a specially earmarked emergency corporate income surtax, which instead of being passed on to consumers in the cost of goods and services might be taken out of dividend payments on a uniform basis. In effect it would be a contribution by shareholders in recognition of services rendered to all American corporations.

Finally, there is the cost of living problem. As nearly as practicable, the retirement funds should, of course, make cost of living adjustments. It might be possible for this money to come from earnings on retirees' accounts and forfeitures. At the point when an employee files a declaration of retirement, his funds would be set aside with the funds of all other retirees. That money would continue to earn interest and the interest would be apportioned among the retirees.

In addition, there could be forfeitures coming from employees who died prior to filing a declaration of retirement without survivors and from some survivors' accounts. Let me explain this very briefly. The proposed system would encourage separate accounts for husbands and wives. Contributions would, of course, be made for working women, but in addition, husbands might be encouraged by a tax deferral to contribute to accounts for wives during periods when they stay home to raise families. Husbands and wives could jointly file a declaration of retirement at any time and receive an annuity based on three-fourths the amount in their combined accounts. The survivor would continue to receive the same amount. (This is merely a variation of a proposal contained in H.R. 1, which may have even greater applicability to the private system than to Social Security, where there are complicating factors.) If husband and wife did not make this election at retirement, the survivor would take an annuity based on his life expectancy and the amount in his account or his spouse's, whichever was larger. All amounts reverting to the fund by reason of a participant's death without a survivor or where the survivor opted to take his own account would be paid over to a Federal pension insurance corporation. The F.P.I.C. would use a portion of this amount to pay off insurance premiums and then at the end of each year would return the balance remaining to the several funds on a pro rata basis according to total assets, to be added to the retirees' cost of living fund. (Until this additional money is available for the purchase of insurance premiums, funds would have authority to borrow from the Treasury.) I leave it to the actuaries among you to determine whether something along these lines would work.

Opposition to this proposal may come far more from its impact on the immense economic power you have amassed over the past twenty years than from any technical objections. 151.8 billion dollars increasing at a rate of more than 13.6 billion a year is a lot of money, and there is very little regulation at all over how it is invested and to what ends.

If this is your only objection to the proposal, I submit that it is untenable at this time in our history. The vote phenomenon in recent primaries is indicative of an impatience on the part of the public with bigness, with the remoteness of decision-making from the citizen, consumer, and taxpayer. There is increasing realization that the investment practices of pension funds are directly and significantly affecting the economic priorities of the nation, that it may be one of the causes of the lack of diversification essential to a healthy competitive economy. At the same time persons covered by pension plans are beginning to express an interest in how the money taken out of their paychecks is being spent.

Pensions are only just beginning to surface as a popular issue. Increasingly, congressmen are coming back to their districts to find that as many persons are concerned about pensions as tax reform and busing. Until now there has been a good deal of discontent, but there has been very little understanding as to the reasons for this discontent. That may change soon. Grossman Publishers will soon be coming out with a small, simple, and eminently readable handbook entitled *You and Your Pension*, authored by myself and Kate Blackwell. It is designed to explain the operation of the private pension system to the millions of persons affected by it, both directly and indirectly, and to outline some suggestions for change and ways for beneficiaries to assert their rights. The book says little you do not already know—it merely synthesizes the volumes of material that somehow haven't yet filtered down to those people most immediately concerned—but you may find it interesting reading.

I suspect that once the public becomes aware of how the system operates its reaction will not differ significantly from that of the 537 persons who responded to a questionnaire that I sent out to 839 people last year. The questionnaire was sent to people who had written to the President, members of Congress, or myself describing their experiences with the private pension system. The responses have been tabulated for a pension report, which I will be submitting on behalf of these people to all members of Congress.

The responses came from forty states. Slightly less than one-half of those answering were retired, about one-third were over sixty-five years of age, and one-fourth were female. More than one-half were receiving or expected to receive private pension benefits.

Not unexpectedly an overwhelming majority—four out of five—said that employer contributions to private pension funds were more like wages than gratuities. More surprisingly, slightly more than one-half said that they would rather see private pension benefits for more people than more money for persons now receiving private pension benefits. All but a very small proportion believe that private pension plans should provide for survivors and should be insured. They would also like to see some sort of vesting. Almost all of these persons are willing to pay the cost of these provisions in terms of reduced benefits. They also are interested in having a voice in who administers the pension fund and where it is invested.

I noticed that your conference literature describes this as the year of decision in employee benefits. You may find that when the time comes for a decision and if and when the public understands the operation of the private pension system, they are going to seek a simple solution. Increasingly, people in Washington who think about these matters are asking the question, Why the private system? Why not an expansion of the Social Security system? And there may not be an effective answer. When persons responding to the questionnaire were asked whether they would rather see higher Social Security retirement benefits for everybody or more people getting private pension benefits, only nine more people opted for the private system than Social Security. This may be a response worth thinking about, especially as more and more disclosures are emerging to persuade them that their complaints reflect, not an aberration, but a system.

APPENDIX D

Employee's Petition to the Defense Department
For Better Pension Protection in the Defense Industry

THE UNITED STATES OF AMERICA
BEFORE THE DEPARTMENT OF DEFENSE

DONALD L. LEDBETTER
   1460 Wake Forest Drive
   Davis, California

ROBERT JOHN EHRLINGER
   10212 Windsor View Drive
   Potomac, Maryland

ARTHUR L. McNEALUS
   287 Fendale Street
   Franklin Square, New York

To the Honorable Melvin R. Laird, Secretary of Defense:

PETITION FOR RULEMAKING

Petitioners respectfully request that the Secretary of Defense direct the issuance of a Revision of the Armed Services Procurement Regulation amending Section 15.205.6(f) to provide that contributions to pension plans will be allowable as items of costs in certain contracts and subcontracts executed or amended on or after October 1, 1971, only to the extent that (1) pension contributions allocable to employees hired on or after October 1, 1971 are used to purchase United States Retirement Plan Bonds in the names of those employees and (2) pension contributions allocable on or after October 1, 1971 to employees hired prior to October 1, 1971 are used to purchase United States Retirement Plan Bonds in the names of those employees if they so elect and affirmatively waive in writing any and all rights they may have to previously accrued but not yet vested pension benefits. Petitioners also request that Respondent require the inclusion of an appropriate clause in all contracts and subcontracts executed or amended on or after October 1, 1971.

The Secretary of Defense has authority to issue the requested Revision pursuant to 5 U.S.C. §301, 10 U.S.C. §§2202, 133(b), A.S.P.R. §§1.101 and 1.105.

Petitioners

1. Petitioner DONALD L. LEDBETTER is a civil/nuclear engineer. He is 45 years old, has worked for defense contractors for more than 18 years and has through no fault of his own been unable to acquire a vested right to a private pension.

Petitioner LEDBETTER was employed by Aerojet Nuclear Systems Company for 8 years as manager of the Computing Services Department. He was laid off on May 29, 1971, along with 75 percent of his company and 100 percent of his department because of a cutback in the NERVA (Nuclear Engine Reactor Vehicle Assembly) contract. The Aerojet Nuclear Systems Company pension plan provides that pension benefits will vest only after 10 years of service.

Petitioner LEDBETTER has also worked for Honeywell Corporation, Westinghouse Atomic Power and for National Gypsum Company. At Honeywell and Westinghouse Atomic Power his employment was terminated because the contract on which he was working was completed. He was laid off by National Gypsum Company when the facility at which he was employed was shut down.

Petitioner LEDBETTER is Chairman of the Industries Section of the National Society of Professional Engineers. He has recently completed a study entitled *Engineer Mobility and Pension Survey.*

2. Petitioner ROBERT JOHN EHRLINGER is an electrical engineer. He is 47 years old and has worked for defense contractors for more than 15 years without acquiring any rights to pension benefits. He has worked for C and S, Inc., Bendix Corporation, Communications Division and Westinghouse Electrical Corporation. He has also done independent research. After a 17 month period of unemployment he is now employed by the Social Security Administration.

Petitioner EHRLINGER believes that action must be taken to change the structure of the defense industry pension system and that his experience with the Bendix Corporation is illustrative of the inherent unfairness of the system. He worked for Bendix for 9 years and 8 months before being laid off because of a loss of research funds. Had he worked for 10 years he would have become entitled to a pension benefit.

3. Petitioner ARTHUR L. McNEALUS is an electronics engineer. He is 53 years old and has worked for defense contractors for 23 years. He was recently laid off from United Aircraft Corporation, Norden Division, where he was Senior Systems Integration Engineer. He was laid off after 15 months of employment owing to a cutback in the F-111 contract. He did not qualify for a pension benefit. He had previously worked for 6 years for Grumman Aerospace where he was laid off during the phase-out of the Apollo contract. He has also worked for Space Technology Laboratories (TRW), Fairchild-Stratos Corporation, Ford Instrument Company and FXR. Despite "liberal" pension plan provisions, petitioner McNealus was not able to qualify for benefits.

Petitioner McNealus has written letters to the President of the United States, his senators and other elected officials requesting that the government take action to secure pension benefits for persons in the defense industry.

The petitioners seek the issuance of the proposed rule on their own behalf and on behalf of all persons similarly situated.

Reasons for Issuing the Proposed Rule

Petitioners have participated and will participate with millions of other employees of defense contractors in pension plans that are as good or better than any industrial pension plans in the United States. According to a recent study, benefit levels in the aerospace industry equal and often exceed those in comparable non-defense industries. In many instances pension benefits vest fully after 10 years and at most require 15 years of service. The vast majority of aerospace plans are fully funded and often overfunded. Pension plans in other defense industries are slightly less liberal but they more than equal plans in similar non-defense industries, Folk, *Pensions and Severance Pay for Displaced Defense Workers,* United States Arms Control and Disarmament Agency Publication E 138, Washington, D.C., U.S. Government Printing Office, 1969. 34–82.

Despite the liberality of defense industry pension plans, a very small percentage of plan participants are receiving or are likely to receive pension benefits from defense industry pension plans.

The Folk study found that 80 percent of the employees in the aerospace industry had less than the 10 years of service required by most plans for vesting. Folk, *supra* at 143. The likelihood that employees of defense contractors will not receive pension benefits has increased sharply since the publication of the Folk study. Recent Bureau of Labor Statistics figures show that layoffs in the aerospace industry have increased 4 times since 1968, from 8.4 percent a year in 1968 to 33.6 percent in the first three months of 1971. Employment in aircraft and parts establishments has decreased from 852,000 persons in 1968 to 689,900 in 1970.

The case histories accompanying the Senate Subcommittee on Labor's March 31, 1971 "Staff Analysis" of 87 pension plans similarly show that an extraordinarily large number of defense workers do not benefit from defense industry pension plans. In Case History Number 38, 20,000 out of the 60,000 employees that had participated in the pension plan since 1957 left the scope of the plan without acquiring vested rights to pension benefits. In Case History Number 52, 66,000 out of 81,000 employees that had left the scope of the plan since 1955 left without acquiring rights to vested benefits. 117 Cong. Rec. 4669 (Daily Ed.)

Petitioner Ledbetter has recently completed a study which shows that engineers, who comprise a substantial portion of defense industry employees, rarely acquire vested rights to pension benefits. The length of job tenure for the engineers sampled in the study averaged 5.7 years. Ledbetter and Gilchrist, *Engineer Mobility and Pension Survey.*

Authority for Issuing the Proposed Rule

Respondent is in a position to provide a less bleak and uncomfortable retirement for millions of defense workers. Respondent can prescribe the terms on which the United States government will pay for employer contributions to pension plans. 10 U.S.C. §2202; 5 U.S.C. §301; A.S.P.R. §§1.101, 1.105. Respondent has already provided that a defense contractor's pension contributions will be allowable items of cost, both in cost reimbursement and fixed price contracts, only if they are "for the exclusive benefit of his employees or their beneficiaries." A.S.P.R. §15.205.6(f), DOD Circular No. 79, May 15, 1970, 26 U.S.C. §401. He can also provide that the United States will pay an employer's pension contributions only if they are for the exclusive benefit of those of his employees *on whose behalf the contributions are made,* or their beneficiaries.

The distinction is crucial. As appears in Part I above, pension contributions do not in fact benefit the vast majority of the defense workers on whose behalf they are made. At best, the contributions benefit the very small proportion of long service employees; at worst—where there are gradual layoffs prior to plan termination—they benefit the employers. At times such as the present, when a substantial curtailment of defense procurement may justify "abnormal reversionary credits," contributions may revert to the Defense Department.

Necessity for Issuing the Proposed Rule

Respondent not only can but should act to guarantee that employees of defense contractors will enjoy a comfortable retirement. He cannot reasonably continue to direct the expenditure of tax revenues for a system that arbitrarily discriminates against persons who have spent their working lives effectuating national defense policy and who, through no fault of their own, are unable to anticipate the vagaries of that policy. He also cannot reasonably await action by the private sector of our economy or Congress.

Neither defense contractors nor labor leaders have come forward with the voluntary arrangements that would provide for immediate vesting and the inter-industry and inter-union pension credit transferability that some see as a solution to the problem of loss of pension benefits.

Defense contractors are, perhaps understandably, not anxious to relinquish a system which enables them to offer high, if illusory, pension benefits to prospective employees and which affords very substantial retirement benefits for company executives along with, in some instances, a secure source of funds from which the contractor can borrow and which can be used for the purchase of corporate stock and bonds. Union leaders are often among the minority of employees who work long enough to be assured of a pension benefit. They would prefer not to remove crucial pension issues from the bargaining table or divest themselves of their often more-than-joint control of pension fund investment decisions. Professional employees are, for the most part, unorganized and without an effective voice to protect their pension benefits.

The Proposed Rule

Petitioners request that Respondent direct that A.S.P.R. 15.205.6(f) be amended as of October 1, 1971, by the addition of the following language immediately after the last sentence of sub-paragraph (2):

> *Provided* that contributions to pension plans paid by contractors are allowable only to the extent that ((a)) contributions allocable to employees hired by the contractor on or after October 1, 1971 are used to purchase United States Retirement Plan Bonds in the names of those employees and ((b)) contributions allocable to employees employed prior to October 1, 1971 are used to purchase United States Retirement Plan Bonds in the names of those employees who elect on or before October 1, 1972 affirmatively to waive in writing any and all rights they may have accrued but not yet vested pension benefits.

Petitioners additionally request that Respondent require the inclusion of the following clause in all contracts and subcontracts executed or amended on or after October 1, 1971:

> The contract price shall not include contributions to pension plans paid by the contractor to pension funds which contributions (a) are allocable to employees hired by the contractor on or after October 1, 1971 unless such contributions are used to purchase United States Retirement Plan Bonds in the names of those employees; (b) are allocable to employees hired prior to October 1, 1971 unless such contributions are used to purchase United States Retirement Plan Bonds in the names of those employees who elect on or before October 1, 1972 affirmatively to waive in writing any and all rights they may have accrued but not yet vested pension benefits.

The Proposed Rule Will Assure That Most
Defense Workers Will Receive Private Pension Benefits

By providing immediate vesting and complete "portability" of pension benefits, the proposed amendment will assure that most defense workers will face retirement with income supplemental to Social Security. It will also guarantee a 5 percent return on their pension investment for employees covered by the amendment, a rate of return equal to, if not exceeding, average pension fund earnings.

The Proposed Rule Is Consistent With A.S.P.R.'s Characterization of Pension Benefits

The proposed amendment is also not inconsistent with the present characterization of pension benefits by A.S.P.R. §20.205.6(f). Section 15.205.6(f)(1) and the proposed amendment both reject the often advanced contentions that pension benefits are a gratuity conferred by employers and/or a "management tool."

Section 15.205.6(f)(1) provides that pension contributions are deferred "remuneration." A.S.P.R. §15.205.6(f)(1). Similarly, the proposed amendment treats pension contributions as amounts that have been earned by providing that they are to be allocated, much as wages are allocated, to individual employees for services rendered.*

Sections 15.205.6(f)(4) and (2) emphasize that pension contributions are allowable only to the extent that they are for services rendered during the contract period and are not conditioned on continued employment with the contractor. A.S.P.R. §§15.205.6(f)(2) and (4). These provisions preclude, as does the proposed amendment, any suggestion that pension contributions may legitimately be used as a means of inducing employees to remain with a contractor.

The Proposed Rule Will Not Be Unduly Burdensome

The proposed amendment can be implemented expeditiously with a minimum of administrative inconvenience. It will provide immediate long-term benefits to employees and will not require the additional expenditure of funds by contractors or the United States government. It will also in no way preclude employers, unions and financial institutions from requesting a further amendment, should they devise an alternative means of assuring adequate retirement income for defense workers at some future date.

* Counsel for petitioners has been advised by the Defense Contract Audit Agency that pension contributions are presently included in overhead and allowed as indirect costs, but that it would not be unduly burdensome were they to be computed as direct costs allocable to defense work done by individual employees.

United States Retirement Plan Bonds

Title 31, United States Code, Sections 757c and 757c-2 and 31 C.F.R. §341 *et seq.* authorizes the issuance of United States Retirement Plan Bonds yielding 5 percent interest. United States Retirement Plan Bonds were first authorized by the Tax Retirement Act of 1962. To date they have been purchased primarily by self-employed persons. The bonds may, however, also be purchased by administrators of qualified pension plans. They must be purchased in the names of plan participants. The bonds are available in denominations of $50, $100, $500 and $1000. Up to $5000 in bonds can be purchased each year for each plan participant. They are redeemable by the owner of the bond at age $59\frac{1}{2}$ years or complete disability, or by a surviving beneficiary designated by the bond owner. 31 C.F.R. §341 *et seq.* The bond owner is free to redeem his bonds at any time after age $59\frac{1}{2}$ when he finds that he needs the retirement income represented by one or more of the bonds. He can also allow the bonds to remain in the Treasury where they will continue to earn interest.

The Proposed Rule Will Not Prejudice the Rights of Defense Workers Who Have Acquired or Will Acquire Vested Rights Under the Present System

Investment of pension contributions in U.S. Retirement Plan Bonds will substantially benefit those employees who have not acquired and do not anticipate that they will acquire vested benefits under present pension arrangements.

Such investment will in no way prejudice the rights of employees who have already acquired vested pension rights, since defense industry pension plans are almost without exception fully funded or overfunded. They have ample assets to meet all accrued liabilities.

Employees who have reason to believe that they will remain with a contractor or in a particular industry long enough to acquire vested rights under the present system will be able to remain under that system. Contributions allocable to those employees will, of course, continue to be paid into the fund in their behalf. In addition, funds to pay their promised benefits will be available from two other sources: (1) amounts forfeited by employees who elect on October 1, 1972 to waive their rights to accrued but not yet vested benefits in exchange for investment of all of their future benefits in U.S. Retirement Plan Bonds and (2) employees who elect on October 1, 1972 to remain in the present system but, contrary to their expectations, subsequently leave the contractor or industry.

The Proposed Rule Will Make It Possible for More Defense Contractors to Provide Pension Benefits

The amendment may encourage smaller businesses who cannot now afford the extensive investment management and other administrative costs of the present system to set up qualified custodial pension plans, thus providing for their employees while also taking advantage of the allowability and deductibility of pension contributions.

Existing Contractual Arrangements Do Not Preclude Issuance of the Proposed Rule

Contractors are in a position to require pension plan administrators to purchase U.S. Retirement Plan Bonds for employees covered by the proposed amendment. In so-called Taft-Hartley Plans, administered pursuant to 29 U.S.C. §186, the contractor and union trustees will have a common interest in persuading the neutral trustee that such investments are appropriate. In other plans, although employers do not, in most instances, formally direct the investment decisions of pension fund administrators, they do have the power to transfer pension funds away from "uncooperative" trustees to administrators whose investment decisions promise to be more satisfactory. This option has been exercised not infrequently to effectuate policies considerably less beneficial to plan participants than investment in 5 percent bonds secured by the credit of the United States.

Pension plans, trust agreements and contracts with administrators can be revised insofar as their provisions are inconsistent with those of the proposed amendment. Collective bargaining agreements will also not bar application of the proposed amendment. Provisions relating to pensions in collective bargaining agreements are tenable only for relatively low turnover situations such as those found in major non-defense industries. Application of those provisions to government contracts which may terminate or be cancelled precipitately is unwarranted. A.S.P.R. §15.205.6(a)(4) specifically provides that

> The application of the provisions of a labor-management agreement designed to apply to a given set of circumstances and conditions of employment . . . is unwarranted when applied to a government contract involving significantly different circumstances and conditions of employment. A.S.P.R. §15.205.6(a)(4).

Conclusion

For the foregoing reasons, petitioners respectfully request that Respondent direct the issuance of the proposed rule.

Respectfully submitted,

DONALD L. LEDBETTER
ROBERT JOHN EHRLINGER
ARTHUR L. McNEALUS

By
   Karen W. Ferguson
   Attorney for Petitioners

1025 15th Street, N.W.
Washington, D.C. 20005

July 14, 1971

APPENDIX E

Ralph Nader's Petition to the
Department of Labor for Better Communication of
Pension Plans to Employees

THE UNITED STATES OF AMERICA
BEFORE THE DEPARTMENT OF LABOR

RALPH NADER
1025 15th St. N.W.
Washington, D.C.

Petitioner.

To The Honorable James D. Hodgson, Secretary of Labor:

PETITION FOR RULEMAKING

Petitioner seeks the issuance of a rule pursuant to the Welfare and Pension Plans Disclosure Act, as amended, 29 U.S.C. §301, *et seq.* ("the Act"), requiring administrators of employee pension benefit plans subject to the provisions of the Act to advise plan participants of circumstances under which they and their survivors will not or may not receive pension benefits.

Petitioner

Petitioner, RALPH NADER, seeks issuance of the proposed rule as an "interested person" within the meaning of the Administrative Procedure Act, 5 U.S.C. 553(e), on behalf of persons who may inadvertently forfeit their right to retirement income from private pensions.

Petitioner has received letters from persons disappointed in their expectation of receiving retirement benefits from private pension plans. These persons have asked petitioner to act to prevent other persons from being similarly disappointed. They have written to petitioner because he is a nationally recognized consumer advocate who has expressed concern about working conditions and the plight of the elderly.

Respondent

Respondent, JAMES D. HODGSON, the Secretary of Labor, is responsible for administering the Act. He is also custodian of thousands of pension complaint letters written to Federal government officials.

The Proposed Rule

The proposed rule, attached hereto as Exhibit A, provides that administrators of pension plans are, where appropriate, to notify pension plan participants in concise and unambiguous "negative" language that they will *not* receive pension benefits based on employer contributions if they fail to satisfy vesting requirements or if there are insufficient funds to pay benefits; that they may *not* receive such benefits if the plan is terminated; that their survivors will *not* be provided for by the plan or will not be provided for absent the exercise of a survivors benefits option; and finally, that they will *not* receive benefits if they do not apply for benefits or do not apply within a specified time period. The language and form of the notice and manner of publication are set forth in the Proposed Rule and appended Notice Form and Sample Notice.

Reasons for Issuing the Proposed Rule

*Plan Descriptions Do Not Put Pension Plan
Participants on Notice That They May Lose Benefits*

1. Letters on file at the Office of Labor-Management and Welfare-Pension Plan Reports of the Department of Labor establish that pension plan participants are often needlessly disappointed in their pension expectations because they are unaware of the conditions that must be satisfied in order for

them to become eligible for pension benefits. The Act provides that descriptions of pension plans must be filed with both the Department of Labor, and the principal office of the plan, and must be communicated to employees at their request. These descriptions are, however, often technical. Usually, they specify only the circumstances under which participants *will* benefit from a pension plan.

The letters reveal that plan participants are frequently unaware that they must work a specified number of years—and often must reach a certain age—to qualify for pension benefits, or that benefits may be forfeited by circumstances such as an extended layoff or a transfer to another union local. Participants assume that employer contributions to pension plans are a part of their wages and will be available, along with Social Security, at retirement.

Plan participants are also frequently unaware that their pension plan may not have sufficient funds to pay promised benefits or that it may be terminated by the sale, relocation, shutdown, merger, or bankruptcy of the company, or for some other reason.

Widows of pension plan participants have written repeatedly to the Federal government to describe their impoverished economic state and to express their shock and disappointment upon discovering that they were not provided for by their husbands' pension plans. It did not occur to most of these women that amounts contributed to the pension plans for their husbands would not pass to them as a part of their husbands' estates. In some instances there was simply no mention of survivors' benefits in the pension plan. In others the provisions were in the plan, but were phrased as a joint and survivors option, and the plan participants were not advised of the necessity for a timely exercise of the option.

Some plan participants lost benefits because they did not know that they must apply for pension benefits within a specified time period and in accordance with prescribed procedures.

2. The impression conveyed by the letters that plan descriptions do not meaningfully disclose to plan participants the limitations and requirements of their pension plan is confirmed by analysis of plan descriptions on file at the Department of Labor.

Petitioner's researcher made a random selection of 10 Plan descriptions published on Department of Labor Form D-1 (and amended Form D-1A) to determine the extent to which those plan descriptions are likely to put participants on notice of the five factors set forth in the proposed rule. The results of the survey appear in the affidavit attached as Exhibit B. They indicate that plan descriptions, including plan booklets, are not designed to put plan participants on notice of the fact that there are circumstances under which they may lose benefits. Rather, they emphasize the circumstances under which participants *will* receive benefits.

3. Petitioner recognizes that efforts are being made by members of the pension industry to develop more effective methods of advising employee-participants of their rights. Accordingly, counsel for petitioner wrote to several firms requesting pension booklets exemplifying the most advanced communications techniques. Five of the booklets received are attached as Exhibit C. These booklets are for the most part more comprehensive and attractive than those reviewed in the above-mentioned survey. They do not, however, differ from the surveyed booklets in their emphasis of the affirmative aspects of plan provisions.

The Secretary Has Authority to Issue the Proposed Rule

Section 5 of the Act provides that pension plan administrators must make plan descriptions available to participants "in such form and detail as the Secretary shall by regulations prescribe." 29 U.S.C. §304. The grant of rule-making authority was deemed to be among the more important amendments added to the Act in 1962. It was designed to give the Secretary full responsibility for insuring "full and accurate disclosure of all pertinent detail" regarding plan operations. S. Rep. No. 908, 87th Cong., 1st Sess. 1 (1961).

To date the Secretary has exercised his rulemaking authority to restate the requirement of Section 6 of the Act (29 U.S.C. §305) that plan descriptions contain specified information (29 C.F.R. §460.2) and to mandate the use of the D-1 or plan description form (29 C.F.R. §460.3), a form used voluntarily for 99 percent of all filings under the Act prior to the issuance of the regulation. (See H.R. Rep. No. 998, 87th Cong., 1st Sess. 34, Minority Views [1961].) The Secretary has authority to do more. As noted by an industry representative opposed to the amendment, the Act "contains no limitation on the extent of detail which the Secretary may require." Hearings on S. 2520 before the Senate and Public Welfare Committee, 87th Cong., 1st Sess. at 106 (July 31, 1961).

The Secretary Must Exercise His Authority to Require Publication of the Additional Detail Specified in the Proposed Rule If *He Is to Effectuate the Purposes of the Act*

Section 2 declares that it is the policy of the Act "to protect . . . the interests of participants in employee welfare and pension benefit plans and their beneficiaries, by requiring the disclosure and reporting to participants and beneficiaries of financial and other information with respect thereto." 29 U.S.C. §301(b). The "other information" referred to in Section 2 is the non-financial information that plan administrators must publish as a part of the plan description:

> the name, address and description of the plan and the type of administration; the schedule of benefits; . . . copies of the plan or of the bargaining agreement, trust agreement, contract or other instrument if any under which the plan was established and is operated; . . . the procedures to be followed in presenting claims for benefits under the plan . . . 29 U.S.C. §305.

Congress mandated publication of this information to "enable the participants and their beneficiaries to acquaint themselves with the benefits provided by the particular plan [and] their rights in respect to such plan. . . ." H.R. Rep. No. 2283, 85th Cong., 2d Sess. 14 (1958).

As demonstrated above, the detail required by the D-1 Form is not adequate to acquaint participants with the contingent nature of their pension rights. The form merely identifies the plan and requires the submission of documents. It is not in any meaningful sense a plan "description." It does not convey a "mental image" of the plan or effectively portray its chief features. See dictionary definitions of "description," *e.g., Webster's New Collegiate Dictionary, Black's Law Dictionary*. Additional detail in the form proposed by petitioner is essential if the disclosure required by the Act is to protect participants' rights in their pension plans.

Additional Reasons for Issuing the Rule

The proposed rule will suggest to plan participants that they should read their plan descriptions with greater care. It may also prompt them to think about retirement before it is too late.

Conclusion

For the foregoing reasons petitioner requests that the Secretary initiate a rulemaking proceeding on the proposed rule within 30 days of receipt of this petition.

Respectfully submitted,

Ralph Nader

Karen W. Ferguson
Attorney for Petitioner
1025 15th St., N.W.
Washington, D.C. 20005
833-9700

SAMPLE NOTICE

SAVE FOR RETIREMENT

To all hourly paid employees:

You will *NOT* receive pension benefits paid for by XYZ Company

> *If* you leave the company before you are 45 years old and before you have worked for the company for a period of 15 years during which you were not discharged or laid off for a period of more than six months.

You will *NOT* receive pension benefits paid for by XYZ Company

> *If* the XYZ Company pension fund does not have enough money to pay benefits either
>
> > When you retire or
> >
> > When the pension fund ends. The XYZ Company reserves the right to terminate the pension fund and distribute accumulated funds.

You may *NOT* receive pension benefits paid for by the XYZ Company

> *If* the XYZ Company is bought, sold, moves to another state, or shuts down for any reason.

Your wife or dependent husband will *NOT* receive pension benefits paid for by the XYZ Company

> *If* you die before you reach age 60, or if you die after age 60 unless you fill out the XYZ Company Survivors Benefit Option form available at the plant personnel office agreeing to take a one-third reduction in your pension benefits in order to give your widow or widower one-half of your pension benefit.

You will *NOT* receive pension benefits paid for by XYZ Company

> *Unless* you apply for benefits in writing to your plant personnel manager within 24 months after you retire.

THERE MAY BE OTHER REASONS WHY YOU WILL NOT RECEIVE PENSION BENEFITS!

READ YOUR PENSION PLAN

Proposed Rule Making*

Office of Labor-Management and Welfare Pension Reports
[29 CFR Part 460]

DESCRIPTION OF EMPLOYEE WELFARE OR PENSION BENEFIT PLANS

Proposed Additional Reporting Requirements

Pursuant to sections 5, 6, and 8 of the Welfare and Pension Plans Disclosure Act, as amended, 72 Stat. 997, 76 Stat. 35, 29 U.S.C. 301 *et seq.* administrators of any welfare or pension benefit plan subject to the Act are required to publish a description of the plan. However, under the existing reporting scheme the Department of Labor has become aware of the fact that many plan participants and beneficiaries of pension plans have difficulty in comprehending the terms of the plan, and their rights as set out in the basic documents under which the plan is established and operated, and which constitute part of the description of the plan. Consequently, many plan participants and beneficiaries are misinformed and mislead as to their rights.

Accordingly, it is proposed herewith to amend the regulations governing the filing of plan descriptions, and the plan description form (Form D-1), to require, with respect to pension plans, additional information which will furnish a comprehensive description of the provisions of plans in a manner calculated to be understood by the average participant or beneficiary. More particularly, the amended plan description will require information as to the eligibility requirements to participate under the plan, the vesting provisions, source(s) and amount of contributions, the benefits provided under the plan, the method by which benefits are computed, procedures to be followed in presenting claims for benefits, and for appealing denial of claims, effect of suspension or termination of contributions, effect of merger or termination of the plan, the provisions governing administration of the plan, a description of the management and investment of plan funds, and other provisions relat-

* Excerpt from Federal Register, Tuesday, February 1, 1972—Volume 37—Number 21

ing to the rights or obligations of participants or beneficiaries.

It is proposed also, that administrators of pension plans who have previously filed a plan description will be required to file a new plan description, or file an amendment to the plan description previously filed, in order that the information referred to herein will be available to participants and beneficiaries of such plans.

Additionally, it is proposed to require administrators of pension benefit plans to notify participants that copies of the description of the plan, and the latest annual report required by section 7 of the Act are available for examination by any participant or beneficiary at the principal office of the plan, and that a copy of the plan description and an adequate summary of the latest annual report will be mailed to a participant or beneficiary on written request. Whenever such plan is amended it is also proposed that administrators must notify participants as to the subject of the amendment(s), that the amendment(s) will be available in the principal office, and will be mailed on written request.

Interested persons are invited to submit written data, views, or comments regarding the proposed rule to the Assistant Secretary of Labor for Labor-Management Relations, U.S. Department of Labor, Washington, D.C. 20210, within 30 days of publication of this notice in the FEDERAL REGISTER.

Copies of the amendatory material to the Form D-1 may be obtained by writing to the Office of Public Information, U.S. Department of Labor, Washington, D.C. 20210. All written materials or suggestions submitted in response to this notice of proposed rule making will be available for public inspection in Room 401, American National Bank Building, 8701 Georgia Avenue, Silver Spring, MD, during regular business hours.

Accordingly, it is proposed herewith to amend 29 CFR Part 460 as follows:

1. The Authority for issuing Part 460 is amended to read as follows:

AUTHORITY: The provisions of this Part 460 issued under sections 5, 6, 7, 8, 72 Stat. 999, 1000, 1002, 76 Stat. 36, 37; 29 U.S.C. 304, 305, 306, 307; Secretary's Order 16–68 (33 F.R. 15574).

2. A new §460.1a is hereby added to 29 CFR Part 460 to read as follows:

§460.1a Notification of availability of plan descriptions and annual reports.

The administrator of any employee pension benefit plan subject to the Welfare and Pension Plans Disclosure Act shall notify the participants of such plan in writing that pursuant to the provisions of section 8 of the Act, participants or beneficiaries are entitled to examine copies of the description of the plan and the latest annual report at the principal office of the plan. Such notice shall identify the location of such office, and the hours during which such reports will be available for examination, and indicate that a copy of the description of the plan and an adequate summary of the annual report will be delivered to a plan participant or beneficiary upon receipt of a written request therefor by the administrator of the plan. Whenever such plan is amended the plan administrator shall cause participants to be notified in writing as to the subject of the amendment(s), and that a copy of the amendment(s) will be made available for examination at the principal office of the plan, or upon written request delivered to a participant or beneficiary.

3. Section 460.2 is amended by designating the existing section as paragraph (a) and adding a paragraph (b) to read as follows:

§460.2 Content of reports—signature or certification.

(b) In addition the administrator of each pension benefit plan shall, as part of the Form D-1 * and in accordance with the instructions contained in the form, file a comprehensive description of the provisions of the plan relating to the eligibility requirements to participate under the plan; vesting provisions, including conditions under which vested benefits may be divested; sources of contributions, amount, periods when due, whether by check off or direct payment; benefits provided under the plan and the method by which they are computed; procedures to be followed in presenting claims for benefits and for appealing denial of claims; the effect of suspension or termination of contributions; the effect of merger or termination of the plan; details as to the administration of the plan; a description of the management and investment of plan funds; and other provisions which relate to the rights or obligations of participants or beneficiaries under the plan. Such information shall be written in a manner calculated to be understood by the average participant or beneficiary. If plan booklets are distributed to participants or beneficiaries such booklets should include the information provided for in this paragraph.

4. Section 460.5 is hereby amended by changing the heading of the section and by adding a new paragraph (c) as follows:

§460.5 Filing plan description amendments.

* Filed as part of the original document.

(c) Administrators of pension plans who have previously submitted a plan description pursuant to §460.2 but which does not include a description of the plan as provided for in paragraph (b) of §460.2 shall submit a revised description of the plan containing information provided for in paragraph (b) of §460.2 on revised Form D-1 incorporating all current information required therein, or shall submit an addendum to the Form D-1 originally filed, containing the information required under paragraph (b) of §460.2 and questions 13 and 14 of the Form D-1 as revised. Such new description or such addendum shall be submitted to the Office of Labor-Management and Welfare-Pension Reports, U.S. Department of Labor, Washington, D.C. 20210, within 120 days after the effective date of this paragraph.

Signed at Washington, D.C., this 27th day of January 1972.

W. J. USERY, JR.,
*Assistant Secretary of Labor
for Labor-Management Relations.*

* *

The proposed rule reprinted above would affect the Labor Department's Form D-1 (Pension Plan Description) by adding Item 13:

ITEM 13. *For Pension Benefit Plans Only.* Attach a comprehensive description of the provisions of the plan. The information furnished shall be written in simple language in a manner calculated to be understood by the average participant or beneficiary. Wherever applicable, emphasize the circumstances under which a participant or beneficiary may not receive benefits (in whole or in part) so as to put him on notice of the fact that there are circumstances under which he may lose benefits or that the payment of vested benefits may commence at normal retirement date or some other time specified in the plan if he quits or is terminated prior to such time.

EXAMPLES:
A participant or beneficiary may be ineligible to receive benefits under a plan for the following reasons:
Because of a break in service
Failure to file a timely claim or appeal for denial of claim
Failure to elect a timely survivor's benefit option

Termination of plan and insufficient funds (no employer guarantee of benefits; benefit payments limited to amount of accumulated plan funds as of the date of termination)

Termination of service prior to normal retirement date (payment of vested benefits not to commence immediately, but at normal retirement date)

The description provided must describe each element of the plan specified in "a" through "j" below.

    a. Eligibility requirements to participate under the plan.
    b. Provisions governing vesting, including conditions under which vested benefits may be divested, if any.
    c. Contributions, including sources, amounts, periods when due and whether by check off or direct payment.
    d. Benefits, including method of computation.
    e. Procedures to be followed in presenting claims for benefits and for appealing denial of claims.
    f. Effect of suspension or termination of contributions.
    g. Effect of merger or termination of plan.
    h. Provisions governing administration of plan.
    i. Management of the plan and investment of plan funds.
    j. Other plan provisions (specify)

CAUTION:

The plan description provided pursuant to Item 13 is intended to explain the plan to participants in an easy-to-understand fashion. In the event of any inconsistency between this description and the actual provisions of the plan, the actual provisions of the plan shall govern.

APPENDIX F

People to Contact

EXECUTIVE BRANCH

THE WHITE HOUSE   Washington, D.C. 20500
President Richard M. Nixon
(202) 456-1414

Peter M. Flanigan, Assistant to the President for International and Economic Policy and Chairman of the President's Committee on Pension Plan Reform Legislation
(202) 456-2361

DEPARTMENT OF LABOR   14th and Constitution Ave., N.W.
Washington, D.C. 20210

James D. Hodgson, Secretary
(202) 961-2001

Laurence H. Silberman, Under Secretary
(202) 961-2005

Labor Management Services Administration
W. J. Usery, Assistant Secretary
Room 3137
(202) 961-2041

Frank M. Kleiler, Deputy Assistant Secretary for Planning and Evaluation
Room 3133
(202) 961-2041

Leonard J. Lurie, Director
8701 Georgia Avenue
Silver Spring, Md. 20210
(202) 393-2420 or 495-4551

Ed Daly, Chief Investigator
8701 Georgia Avenue
Silver Spring, Md. 20210
(202) 393-2420

Bureau of Labor Statistics General Accounting Office
441 G St., N.W.
Washington, D.C. 20250

Donald M. Landay, Division Chief, Division of General Compensation Structures
Room 4071
(202) 961-2160

DEPARTMENT OF THE TREASURY 15th and Pennsylvania Ave., N.W.
Washington, D.C. 20220

Office of Tax Policy
Edwin S. Cohen, Assistant Secretary
Room 3430
(202) 964-5561

Joel Segall, Assistant to Cohen
(202) 964-2563

Internal Revenue Service 12th and Constitution Ave., N.W.
Washington, D.C. 20220

Isidore Goodman, Chief, Pension Trust Branch

Room 6229
(202) 964-3871

DEPARTMENT OF HEALTH, EDUCATION AND WELFARE 330 Independence Ave., S.W.
Washington, D.C. 20201

Social Security Administration
Walter W. Kolodrubetz, Office of Research and Statistics
HEW North, Room 3072
(202) 962-8083
Patience Lauriat
(202) 962-4667

DEPARTMENT OF JUSTICE Constitution between 9th and 10th Streets, N.W.
Washington, D.C. 20530

Charles Ruff, Chief, Management and Labor Section, Criminal Division
Room 1333
(202) 739-3761

NATIONAL LABOR RELATIONS BOARD 1717 Pennsylvania Ave., N.W.
Washington, D.C. 20570

Edward B. Miller, Chairman
Room 630
(202) 382-4770

SECURITIES AND EXCHANGE COMMISSION 500 N. Capitol St., N.W.
Washington, D.C. 20570

Alan B. Levenson, Director, Division of Corporate Finance
Room 616
(202) 755-1136
Jeannette Honsa, Financial Economist
(202) 755-1660

CONGRESS

General Subcommittee on Labor, Senate Committee on Labor and Public Welfare
New Senate Office Building, Room G-237, Washington, D.C.
(202) 225-3674
Senator Harrison A. Williams, Jr. (D-N.J.), Chairman

General Subcommittee on Labor Study Group on Pension Plans
Mario Noto, Special Counsel
Old Senate Office Building, Room 352, Washington, D.C.
(202) 225-3656
Michael Gordon, Minority Counsel
New Senate Office Building, Room 4226, Washington, D.C.
(202) 225-2705

Senate Committee on Finance
New Senate Office Building, Room 2227, Washington, D.C.
(202) 225-4515
Senator Russell B. Long (D-La.), Chairman

General Subcommittee on Labor, House Committee on Education and Labor
Rayburn House Office Building, Room B345D, Washington, D.C.
(202) 225-5331
Rep. John H. Dent (D-Pa.), Chairman

General Subcommittee on Labor Pension Task Force
Cannon House Office Building, Room 112, Washington, D.C.
(202) 225-5495
Vance Anderson, Majority Counsel

House Committee on Ways and Means
Longworth House Office Building, Room 1102, Washington, D.C.
(202) 225-3625
Rep. Wilbur D. Mills (D-Ark.), Chairman

Room 6229
(202) 964-3871

DEPARTMENT OF HEALTH, EDUCATION AND WELFARE 330 Independence Ave., S.W.
Washington, D.C. 20201

Social Security Administration
Walter W. Kolodrubetz, Office of Research and Statistics
HEW North, Room 3072
(202) 962-8083
Patience Lauriat
(202) 962-4667

DEPARTMENT OF JUSTICE Constitution between 9th and 10th Streets, N.W.
Washington, D.C. 20530

Charles Ruff, Chief, Management and Labor Section, Criminal Division
Room 1333
(202) 739-3761

NATIONAL LABOR RELATIONS BOARD 1717 Pennsylvania Ave., N.W.
Washington, D.C. 20570

Edward B. Miller, Chairman
Room 630
(202) 382-4770

SECURITIES AND EXCHANGE COMMISSION 500 N. Capitol St., N.W.
Washington, D.C. 20570

Alan B. Levenson, Director, Division of Corporate Finance
Room 616
(202) 755-1136
Jeannette Honsa, Financial Economist
(202) 755-1660

CONGRESS

General Subcommittee on Labor, Senate Committee on Labor and Public Welfare
New Senate Office Building, Room G-237, Washington, D.C.
(202) 225-3674
Senator Harrison A. Williams, Jr. (D-N.J.), Chairman

General Subcommittee on Labor Study Group on Pension Plans
Mario Noto, Special Counsel
Old Senate Office Building, Room 352, Washington, D.C.
(202) 225-3656
Michael Gordon, Minority Counsel
New Senate Office Building, Room 4226, Washington, D.C.
(202) 225-2705

Senate Committee on Finance
New Senate Office Building, Room 2227, Washington, D.C.
(202) 225-4515
Senator Russell B. Long (D-La.), Chairman

General Subcommittee on Labor, House Committee on Education and Labor
Rayburn House Office Building, Room B345D, Washington, D.C.
(202) 225-5331
Rep. John H. Dent (D-Pa.), Chairman

General Subcommittee on Labor Pension Task Force
Cannon House Office Building, Room 112, Washington, D.C.
(202) 225-5495
Vance Anderson, Majority Counsel

House Committee on Ways and Means
Longworth House Office Building, Room 1102, Washington, D.C.
(202) 225-3625
Rep. Wilbur D. Mills (D-Ark.), Chairman

APPENDIX F   195

GENERAL

AFL-CIO
815 15th St., N.W., Washington, D.C. 20006
(202) 293-5000
Andrew J. Biemiller, Legislative Director

American Bankers Association
1120 Connecticut Ave., N.W., Washington, D.C. 20036
(202) 467-4251

American Enterprise Institute for Public Policy Research
1200 17th St., N.W., Washington, D.C. 20036
(202) 296-5616

American Pension Conference
358 Fifth Avenue, New York, N.Y. 10001
(212) 695-0679

Association of Private Pension and Welfare Plans, Inc.
1028 Connecticut Ave., N.W., Washington, D.C. 20036
(202) 659-8274
Joseph P. Leary, Executive Director

Merton C. Bernstein, Professor of Law
Ohio State University, Columbus, Ohio 43210
(614) 422-2631

Brookings Institute
1775 Massachusetts Ave., N.W., Washington, D.C. 20036
(202) 483-8919

Eastern Conference of Health, Welfare and Pension Plans, Inc.
150 Fifth Avenue, New York, N.Y. 10011
(212) 924-0282

International Brotherhood of Teamsters
25 Louisiana Ave., N.W., Washington, D.C. 20001
(202) 783-0525
David A. Sweeney, Political and Legislative Director

Midwest Pension Conference
1 First National Plaza, Chicago, Ill. 60670
(312) 786-5242

National Association of Manufacturers
1133 15th St., N.W., Washington, D.C. 20005
(202) 833-1800

National Council of Senior Citizens
1511 K Street, N.W., Washington, D.C. 20005
(202) 783-6850
Rudolph T. Danstedt, Assistant to the President

National Foundation of Health, Welfare and Pension Plans
P.O. Box 69, Brookfield, Wis. 53005
(414) 786-6700

National Retired Teachers Association
1225 Connecticut Ave., N.W., Washington, D.C. 20036
(202) 659-4670

National Society of Professional Engineers Pension Study Group
2029 K Street, N.W., Washington, D.C. 20006
(202) 337-0420

Pension Research Council, Wharton School of Finance and Commerce
Deitrich Hall
University of Pennsylvania
Philadelphia, Pa. 19104
(215) 594-7601

Southern Pension Conference
c/o Hansell, Post, Brandon & Dorsey
First National Bank Building, Atlanta, Ga. 30303
(404) 525-3558

Teachers Insurance and Annuity Association
730 Third Avenue, New York, N.Y. 10017
(212) 697-7600

United Auto Workers Union
1126 16th Street, N.W., Washington, D.C. 20036
(202) 296-7484
John Beidler, Legislative Director

United Steelworkers of America
1001 Connecticut Avenue, N.W., Washington, D.C. 20036
(202) 638-6929
Jack Sheehan, Legislative Director

Western Pension Conference
c/o Bank of America
Employee Benefit Trust Department 9260
P.O. Box 37,000, San Francisco, Calif. 94137
(415) 622-2210

NOTES

Chapter I

1. Dan McGill, *Fulfilling Pension Expectations*, Pension Research Council of the Wharton School of Finance and Commerce, University of Pennsylvania (February, 1962), p. 299. *(Emphasis added.)*

Chapter II

1. From a letter to us in response to our questionnaire. Hereafter quotes from employees taken from letters sent to us will not be footnoted. Names have been changed.
2. *Preliminary Report of the Private Welfare and Pension Plan Study, 1971*, the Committee on Labor and Public Welfare, Subcommittee on Labor, U.S. Senate, 92d Cong., 1st Sess. (Washington, U.S. Government Printing Office, 1971). See also Senator Javits' remarks in *Pensions* magazine (Winter, 1972), p. 115.
3. James H. Schulz, *Pension Aspects of the Economics of Aging: Present and Future Roles of Private Pensions*, prepared for the Special Committee on Aging, U.S. Senate (Washington, U.S. Government Printing Office, 1970), pp. 38–39.
4. *Private Welfare and Pension Plan Legislation*, Hearings, General Subcommittee on Labor, Committee on Education and Labor, U.S. House of Representatives, 92d Cong., 1st and 2d Sess. (Washington, U.S. Government Printing Office, 1970), p. 262.

5. Hearings, Subcommittee on Labor, U.S. Senate (1968), exhibit A-13.
6. Dick Barnes, the Associated Press, second in series (July 14, 1970).
7. Dan McGill, *Fulfilling Pension Expectations*, Pension Research Council of the Wharton School of Finance and Commerce, University of Pennsylvania (February, 1962), p. 83.
8. Hearings, General Subcommittee on Labor, U.S. House of Representatives, *op. cit.*, p. 465.
9. McGill, *op. cit.*, p. 5.
10. Thomas R. Donahue, Hearings, Subcommittee on Labor, U.S. Senate (February 17, 1968).
11. Merton C. Bernstein, Hearings, Subcommittee on Labor, U.S. Senate (1968).

Chapter III

1. In a report to the Joint Economic Committee a team of economists has noted that "although private pensions cover fewer workers than the public system, they are a significant element in the nation's total retirement program. For OASDHI beneficiaries in receipt of such pensions, the supplementary benefit means the difference between a less than modest and a reasonably comfortable level of living." Elizabeth M. Heidbreder, Walter W. Kolodrubetz, and Alfred Skolnik, "Old Age Programs," *Old Age Income Assurance*, Part II, U.S. Joint Economic Committee (Washington, U.S. Government Printing Office, 1968), p. 52094.
2. *Social Security Bulletin*, Vol. 35, No. 4 (April, 1972), p. 1. A 20 percent increase will be reflected in checks mailed after October 2, 1972.
3. *Interim Report of Activities of the Private Welfare and Pension Plan Study, 1971*, Committee on Labor and Public Welfare, U.S. Senate, Subcommittee on Labor, 92d Cong., 1st Sess. (Washington, U.S. Government Printing Office, 1972), p. 66.
4. Merton C. Bernstein, *The Future of Private Pensions* (New York, The Free Press of Glencoe, 1964), p. 10.
5. Brother Cornelius Justin, F.S.C. and Mario E. Impellizeri, "The Mirage of Private Pensions," reprinted in *Hearings*, General Subcommittee on Labor, U.S. House of Representatives (1970), p. 388.
6. *Ibid.*, p. 390.
7. James H. Schulz, *Pension Aspects of the Economics of Aging; Present and Future Roles of Private Pensions*, prepared for the Special Committee on Aging, U.S. Senate (Washington, U.S. Government Printing Office, January, 1970), p. 7.
8. Bernstein, *op. cit.*
9. *Ibid.*
10. *Ibid.*, p. 13.
11. Schulz, *op. cit.*
12. Bernstein, *op. cit.*, pp. 12–13.

Chapter IV

1. Merton Bernstein has summed up the inadequacy of the insurance model for private pensions in a speech to the American Enterprise Institute Symposium on Private Pensions and the Public Interest, May 9, 1969: "When these hazards (old age, early retirement, disability, death protection, income, and living standards) are described, it becomes clear that the insurance model, shifting resources from all to the minority who attain benefit eligibility, is inappropriate to pension plans because *most* plan participants are not merely subject to the hazards, they (and their dependents) *will* actually suffer the losses. So long as private plans *by design* limit benefit eligibility to a minority of plan participants, they will fail to satisfy their purposes."
2. Dan McGill, *Fulfilling Pension Expectations*, Pension Research Council of the Wharton School of Finance and Commerce, University of Pennsylvania (February, 1962), p. 83.
3. *Ibid.*, p. 9.
4. *Ibid.*, p. 206.
5. *Ibid.*, p. 51.
6. *Ibid.*, pp. 209–210.
7. *Ibid.*, p. 83.

Chapter V

1. *Monthly Labor Review* (July, 1970), p. 45. No data are available showing the qualifying requirements for all private pension plans. A study published in the *Monthly Labor Review* (July, 1970), covering some 1433 plans on file with the U.S. Department of Labor, reported the requirements of these plans as of 1969. Based on these plans, of one hundred workers entering covered employment at age twenty-five, thirty-one would gain a nonforfeitable pension right in ten years; fifty-one would gain a nonforfeitable pension right after fifteen years; only fifty-seven of the original one hundred would gain nonforfeitable rights after twenty years.
2. *Ibid.* Recent studies indicate that about three-fourths of all covered workers had some kind of vesting provisions in their plans by the end of 1969. Vesting is far more prevalent in some industries than in others. Nearly four-fifths of the workers in manufacturing, communications, public utilities, finance, insurance, and real estate have vesting. Vesting is least common in mining (34 percent), transportation (46 percent), and services (53 percent).
3. *Ibid.*, page 54.
4. *Preliminary Report of the Private Welfare and Pension Plan Study, 1971*, Committee on Labor and Public Welfare, Subcommittee on Labor, U.S. Senate (Washington, U.S. Government Printing Office, 1971). The study was made by A. S. Hansen, Inc., and included only plans serviced by the company.

5. Hearings, Labor Subcommittee, U.S. Senate (1968).
6. Merton C. Bernstein, *The Future of Private Pensions* (New York, The Free Press of Glencoe, 1964), p. 261.
7. James H. Schulz, *Pension Aspects of the Economics of Aging: Present and Future Roles of Private Pensions*, prepared for the Special Committee on Aging, U.S. Senate (Washington, U.S. Government Printing Office, January, 1970), p. 39.
8. Noel Arnold Levin, *Labor-Management Benefit Funds* (New York, Practicing Law Institute, 1971).
9. *Gaydosh v. Lewis*, 410 F.2d. 262 (D.C. Cir., 1969).
10. *McCostis v. Nashua Pressmen Union*, 109 N.H. 226, 248 A.2d 885 (1968).
11. *Kosty v. Lewis*, 319 F.2d 744 (D.C. Cir., 1963), cert.denied, 375 U.S. 964 (1964). *Collins V. U.M.W. Welfare and Retirement Fund*, 298 F. Supp. 964 (D.D.C., 1969).
12. Levin, *op. cit.*, for discussion of court trends.

Chapter VI

1. *Monthly Labor Review* (September, 1968).
2. Merton C. Bernstein, *The Future of Private Pensions* (New York, The Free Press of Glencoe, 1964), p. 52.
3. Hugh Folk, *Pensions and Severance Pay for Displaced Defense Workers*, U.S. Arms Control and Disarmament Agency, Publication E 138 (Washington, U.S. Government Printing Office, 1969), pp. 34–82.
4. Bernstein, *op. cit.*, page 9. In 1967, for example, 1832 manufacturing firms folded, 1246 wholesale concerns, 2261 construction companies, 1329 service firms, and 5696 retail outlets.
5. *Ibid.*
6. *Ibid.*, p. 8.
7. *Ibid.*, p. 10.
8. *Ibid.*, p. 11.
9. *Ibid.*, p. 94.
10. *Ibid.*, page 116. Also see Bernstein's testimony before the General Subcommittee on Labor, House of Representatives, March 12, 1970, for his discussion of "actuarial gain." Also see *Gorr v. Consolidated Foods Corporation*, 253 Minn. 375, 91 N.W. 2d 772 (1958).
11. *Ibid.*
12. Noel Arnold Levin, *Labor-Management Benefit Funds* (New York, Practicing Law Institute, 1971), p. 237.
13. *Ibid.*, pp. 237–238.

Chapter VII

1. *Private Welfare and Pension Plan Study, 1971*, Hearings, Committee on Labor and Public Welfare, Subcommittee on Labor, U.S. Senate, 92d Cong. 1st. Sess. (July 27, 28, 29, 1971), Part I, p. 340.

2. Second in Associated Press series (July 14, 1970).
3. Emerson Beier, "Terminations of Pension Plans: 11 Years' Experience," 90 *Monthly Labor Review*, No. 6 (June 26, 1967).
4. Jacob C. Hurwitz and Willie L. Burris, *Study of the Termination of UAW Pension Plans*, UAW Social Security Department (October 7, 1970). Detailed information was available for forty plans covering a total of 26,254 workers when terminated. The study was based on data from these forty plans.
5. *Ibid.*, p. 4.
6. Merton C. Bernstein, *The Future of Private Pensions* (New York, The Free Press of Glencoe, 1964), p. 94.
7. *Interim Report of Activities of the Private Welfare and Pension Plan Study, 1971*, Report, Committee on Labor and Public Welfare, Subcommittee on Labor, U.S. Senate, 92d Cong., 1st Sess. (Washington, U.S. Government Printing Office, February 22, 1971), pp. 80–81.
8. Letter to Congress quoted in *Washington Report*, UAW Citizenship-Legislative Department, Vol. 10, No. 28 (July 20, 1970).
9. Testimony before the General Subcommittee on Labor, House of Representatives, April 21, 1971.
10. Dan McGill, *Fulfilling Pension Expectations*, Pension Research Council of the Wharton School of Finance and Commerce, University of Pennsylvania (February, 1962), p. 276.
11. Warren Berry, "Washington Views the Pension Scene," *Institutional Investor: The Journal for Professional Money Managers* (August, 1971), pp. 46–47.

Chapter VIII

1. Dick Barnes, Associated Press, fourth in series (July 16, 1970), based on an AP study and Justice Department files.
2. Charles Ruff, Chief, Management and Labor Section, Criminal Division, U.S. Department of Justice.
3. Statement by Senator Homer E. Capehart, appointed permanent Receiver of the Barbers, Beauticians and Allied Industries Pension Fund, July 7, 1971.
4. Barnes, *op. cit.*
5. Ed Daly, investigator, Welfare and Pension Plans Division, Department of Labor, Washington, D.C.
6. The Teamsters' Pension Fund case has also been extensively reported in the press. See AP series by Dick Barnes, third in series (July 15, 1970). Also see series by reporters Jeff Morgan and Gene Ayres in the *Oakland Tribune* (September 21–28, 1969); inserted in the *Congressional Record*, Vol. 115, No. 192 (Thursday, November 20, 1969), pp. S 14713–S 14722.
7. *Private Welfare and Pension Plan Legislation*, Hearings, General Subcommittee on Labor, Committee on Education and Labor, House of Representatives, 92d Cong., 1st and 2d Sess. (Washington, U.S. Government Printing Office, 1970), p. 475.

8. Dick Barnes, Associated Press, third in series (July 15, 1970).
9. *Private Welfare and Pension Plan Study, 1971*, Hearings, Committee on Labor and Public Welfare, Subcommittee on Labor, U.S. Senate, 92d Cong., 1st Sess., Part II (Washington, U.S. Government Printing Office, 1971), p. 440.
10. *Ibid.,* p. 516.
11. *Ibid.,* p. 599.
12. Report, *Council of Profit-Sharing Industries*, Vol. 19, No. 1 (January, 1971).
13. Hearings, Subcommittee on Labor, U.S. Senate, p. 861ff.
14. Dick Barnes, Associated Press, first in series (July 13, 1970).
15. *Ibid.*
16. *Interim Report of Activities of the Private Welfare and Pension Plan Study, 1971*, Committee on Labor and Public Welfare, Subcommittee on Labor, U.S. Senate, 92d Cong., 1st Sess. (Washington, U.S. Government Printing Office, February 22, 1972), p. 165.
17. Dick Barnes, Associated Press, first in series (July 13, 1970).
18. *Securities and Exchange Commission Statistical Series*, Release No. 2581 (April 4, 1972).
19. *Ibid.*
20. *Securities and Exchange Commission Statistical Series*, Release No. 2564 (December 30, 1971). In the same year, of the assets of private noninsured pension funds, 1.9 percent was in cash and deposits, 3.1 percent in U.S. Government securities, 1.8 percent in preferred stock, 4.4 percent in mortgages, and 4.9 percent in other assets.
21. *Ibid.*
22. Lawrence D. Jones, *Bank Trust Activity and the Public Interest*, prepared for the Commission on Financial Structure and Regulation (June, 1971), p. 5.
23. *Ibid.,* pp. 7–8.
24. *Pension Funds: Newest Among Major Financial Institutions*, prepared for the Commission on Financial Structure and Regulation (March, 1971).
25. Jones, *op. cit.,* p. 25. Also Murray, *op. cit.,* p. 12.
26. *Securities and Exchange Commission Statistical Series*, Release No. 2599 (June 20, 1972). This rate of return excludes net realized gain on sale of assets and compares to a rate of return of 4.1 percent in 1970.
27. *Institutional Investor: The Journal for Professional Money Managers* (August, 1971) p. 21.

Chapter IX

1. Walter W. Kolodrubetz, "Private and Public Retirement Pensions: Findings from the 1968 Survey of the Aged," *Social Security Bulletin* (September, 1970), p. 7.
2. *Ibid.,* p. 6.
3. *Interim Report of Activities of the Private Welfare and Pension Plan Study, 1971*, Committee on Labor and Public Welfare, Subcommittee on Labor, U.S. Senate, 92d

Cong., 1st Sess. (Washington, U.S. Government Printing Office, 1972), pp. 65–66.
4. *Ibid.*
5. *Ibid.*
6. Walter W. Kolodrubetz, "Two Decades of Employee-Benefit Plans, 1950–70: A Review," *Social Security Bulletin* (April, 1972), p. 19.
7. Kolodrubetz, "Private and Public Retirement Pensions: Findings from the 1968 Survey of the Aged," *op. cit.*, p. 7. The Social Security Administration reports that in 1967 one-third of the benefits from private pensions were in the range of $500 to $999; two-thirds were between $300 and $1499.
8. *Pittsburgh Plate Glass Co. v. National Labor Relations Board*, December, 1971.
9. Kolodrubetz, "Two Decades of Employee-Benefit Plans, 1950–70: A Review," *op. cit.*, p. 21. These figures represent a 14 percent increase in benefit payments and a 13 percent increase in number of beneficiaries over 1969. A major reason for the increase in beneficiaries that year was widespread unemployment with its pressures for retirement. Increase in beneficiaries also reflects the fact that more people, brought under coverage of private pensions during their big growth in the 1950's, are now reaching retirement age.
10. *Ibid.*, p. 19.
11. Dan McGill, *Fulfilling Pension Expectations*, Pension Research Council of the Wharton School of Finance and Commerce, University of Pennsylvania (February, 1962), p. 71.
12. "Job Tenure," *Monthly Labor Review*, September, 1969, pp. 18–19. The survey showed the following:

Median Years on Current Job

	All Persons	
Age	Men	Women
30–34	3.9	1.8
35–39	5.8	2.6
40–44	8.4	3.2
45–49	10.2	4.4
50–54	12.6	6.2
55–59	14.7	8.2
60–64	15.1	9.4

Median Years—Selected Occupations

	Men by Age		Women by Age	
	24–44	45 yrs over	24–44	45 yrs over
Manufacturing				
Durable Goods	4.5	14.3	2.4	8.3
Nondurable Goods	5.3	15.4	2.8	9.1
Wholesale & Retail				
Trade	3.3	8.8	1.5	4.9
Operatives & Kindred				
Workers	3.8	12.8	2.1	7.7

13. *Ryan School Retirement Trust v. Commissioner*, 24 T.C. 127 (1955). The Commissioner acquiesced in the decision, 1955-2 *Cum. Bull.* 9. See Merton C. Bernstein, *The Future of Private Pensions*, p. 204.
14. "Interim Report," *op. cit.*, pp. 65–66.
15. *Private Welfare and Pension Plan Study, 1971*, Hearings, Committee on Labor and Public Welfare, Subcommittee on Labor, U.S. Senate, Part II, 92d Cong., 1st Sess. (Washington, U.S. Government Printing Office, 1971), p. 809.

Chapter X

1. John McConnell, "Role of Public and Private Programs in Old Age Assurance," *Old Age Income Assurance*, Part I, Joint Economic Committee, 90th Cong., 1st Sess. (Washington, U.S. Government Printing Office, 1968), p. 45.
2. *Social Security Bulletin*, Vol. 35, No. 4 (April, 1972), p. 1.
3. *Economics of Aging: Toward a Full Share in Abundance*, Hearings, Special Committee on Aging, U.S. Senate, 92d Cong., 1st Sess., Part 1, Survey Hearing (Washington, U.S. Government Printing Office, 1969), p. 217. (Emphasis added.)
4. Emerson Beier, "Incidence of Private Retirement Plans," *Monthly Labor Review* (July, 1971), p. 37.
5. *Ibid.*
6. James H. Schulz, *Pension Aspects of the Economics of Aging: Present and Future Roles of Private Pensions*, working paper prepared for the Special Committee on Aging, U.S. Senate, (Washington, U.S. Government Printing Office, 1970), p. 26.
7. Harry E. Davis and Arnold Strasser, "Private Pension Plans, 1960 to 1969—An Overview," *Monthly Labor Review* (July, 1970), p. 47.
8. Elizabeth M. Heidbreder, Walter Kolodrubetz and Alfred M. Skolnik, "Old Age Programs," *Old Age Income Assurance*, Part VI, Joint Economic Committee (Washington, U.S. Government Printing Office, 1968), p. 37.
9. *Ibid.*

10. Beier, *op. cit.*, pp. 37–40. The B.L.S. reported that in establishments with average pay below $2.50 an hour, eight out of ten employees were in groups without retirement expenditures in 1968. In firms with average hourly wages of $5 or more, only two out of ten employees were in groups without expenditures for retirement.

    Similarly, only 18 percent of the employees in unionized groups were without retirement expenditures, compared with 56 percent of those in nonunion situations. The B.L.S. found, however, that unions whose members worked for low wages "apparently chose to place higher priority on current wages than on deferred retirement income." Thus where wages were below $2.50 an hour, 59 percent of the employees in unionized groups were without pension coverage. As wage levels rose, so did the percentage of those with coverage until only 6 percent were without coverage when compensation was $5 an hour or more.

    The same patterns exist in comparing pension coverage for employees in large and in small firms. 73 percent of those in firms with fewer than one hundred workers were in groups with no retirement expenditures. (One-half the nation's private work force was employed in such units in 1968.) Only 7 percent had no retirement expenditures when there were 500 employees or more.
11. *Ibid.*, p. 40. (Emphasis added.)
12. Schulz, *op. cit.*, pp. 27–30.
13. *Ibid.*, p. 27. 163,000 persons were added to self-employed coverage in 1968 alone, compared to a total of 84,000 in the prior five years.
14. *Ibid.* Data from the 1965 business income tax returns indicate that only 18 percent of all retirement plans covering self-employed proprietors also included employees in the plan. Out of 30,781 plans covering proprietors, employees participated in only 5457.
15. *Economics of Aging: Toward a Full Share in Abundance, op. cit.*, p. 196.
16. Eugene Loren and Thomas Barker, *Survivor Benefits* (Detroit, Michigan Health and Social Security Research Institute, 1968).
17. "Pension Plans Under Collective Bargaining: Benefits for Survivors, Winter 1961–62," *B.L.S. Bulletin*, No. 1334, 1962. "Digest of 100 Selected Pension Plans Under Collective Bargaining, Spring 1968," *B.L.S. Bulletin* No. 1597 (February, 1969). Also see *Economics of Aging*, p. 221. Under most bargained plans in a 1962 study, the worker had to give up one-fifth of his pension to provide his wife with one-half of the reduced benefit.
18. Schulz, *op. cit.*, p. 33.
19. The Tool and Die Plan, as reported by James Brindle, director, Social Security Department of the United Auto Workers, at the 15th annual conference of the Council on Employee Benefits. See Merton Bernstein, *The Future of Private Pensions*, p. 33, fn. 48.
20. Meyer Melnikoff, Senior Vice President and Actuary of Prudential Insurance Company, "Survivors Benefits," *Pension Sessions: Trends in Pension Benefits* (1965), pp. 133–136.
21. Schulz, *op. cit.*, p. 34.
22. Heidbreder et al., *op. cit.*, p. 37.

23. *Tax Proposals Affecting Private Pension Plans*, Hearings, before the House Committee on Ways and Means, Part 2 (Washington, U.S. Government Printing Office, May 10, 11, 12, 1972), p. 406.
24. See testimony of Manuel F. Cohen before the Senate Subcommittee on Labor of the Senate Committee on Labor and Public Welfare, June 21, 1972.
25. Lawrence D. Jones, *Bank Trust Activity and the Public Interest*, prepared for the Commission on Financial Structure and Regulation (June, 1971), pp. 7–8.
26. *Ibid.*, p. 10.
27. Roger F. Murray, *Pension Funds: Newest Among Major Financial Institutions*, prepared for the Commission on Financial Structure and Regulation (March, 1971), p. 12.
28. *The Penn Central Failure and the Role of Financial Institutions*, Part V, Staff Report of the House Committee on Banking and Currency, 92d Cong., 1st Sess. (Washington, U.S. Government Printing Office, 1971), March 29, 1971.
29. *Ibid.*, p. iv.

Chapter XI

1. Testimony before the Subcommittee on Labor, U.S. Senate, June 14, 1972.
2. *Ibid.*
3. Hearings, June 20, 1972.
4. *Ibid.*
5. Andrew J. Biemiller, director, Department of Legislation, AFL-CIO *Tax Proposals Affecting Private Pension Plans*, Hearings, House Committee on Ways and Means, 92d Cong., 2d Sess., Part 2 (May 10, 11, 12, 1972), p. 403.
6. *Op. cit.*

Chapter XII

1. *Private Welfare and Pension Plan Legislation*, Hearings, General Subcommittee on Labor, Committee on Education and Labor, House of Representatives, 91st Cong., 1st and 2d Sess. (Washington, U.S. Government Printing Office, 1970), p. 816.
2. E. S. Willis, representing the U.S. Chamber of Commerce, *ibid.*, p. 538.
3. *Ibid.*, p. 700.

Index

Abel, I. W., 62
actuarial gains, 52
actuary, job of pension, 22–4, 28
Advisory Council on Employee Welfare and Pension Benefit Plans, 159
Aerojet Nuclear Systems Company, 170
aerospace industry and pension plans, 6–7, 48–9, 172
AFL-CIO, 128, 195
agents, pension, 21
agricultural workers' exclusion from pensions, 94
Amalgamated Clothing Workers of America, 56
American Bankers Association, 128, 161, 195
American Federation of Labor (A.F. of L.), 15, 36; *see also* AFL-CIO
American Institute of Certified Public Accountants Accounting Principles Board, 26
American Pension Conference, 128, 195
American Telephone & Telegraph, 86
amount of money an individual can expect to collect from a private pension, 79–91
annuity pension plan, proposed, 124–6, 158–68
Apollo contract, 48
Armour & Company, 46
A. S. Hansen, Inc., 34 n.
Associated Press, 89
Association of Private Pension and Welfare Plans, Inc., 128, 161, 195
automatic death benefits under private pension plans, 97 n., 99–100

Baldwin-Lima-Hamilton Company, 45–6
Ballantine Brewery, 121
bankruptcy and pension plans, 24, 46, 47, 105–6
banks' handling of pension funds, 76–8
Barnes, Dick, 58

Battle Creek, Michigan, 12
Beidler, John, 197
Beier, Emerson, 94–5
Bendix Corporation, 171
benefits collected under private pensions, 79–91; basis of, 81–3 and passim
Bernstein, Merton C., 59 n., 195; on pension payoffs, 11; on Williams-Javits bill, 117; on 100 percent vesting of all credits, 118; on Nixon "rule of fifty," 120–1; on Social Security, 122–3
Biemiller, Andrew J., 195
blacks, minority groups, and pension plans, 84
Blankenship et al. v. Boyle et al., 70–1
Block, Max, Jr., 67
Boeing Aircraft, 84
Boyle, W. A., 70
Bradshaw, Jane, 12–13
Brock, John, 47–8
Brookings Institute, 195
Buena Park, California, 6
Bureau of Labor Statistics (B.L.S.), 58 n.–59 n., 80, 93, 94, 97 n., 172, 192
business shutdowns and pension plans, 46, 47, 49–50, 118

C and S, Inc., 171
California, 6, 48
Carney, Charles J., 157
central pension commission, proposed, 120, 154–5
changing jobs, pension plans and the problem of, 36–8, 117, 160
Charles D. Spencer and Associates, Inc., 59 n.
Chase Manhattan Bank, 105–6
Chicago, 46, 51, 67, 72
Cleveland, 7
coal industry, 4–5, 71
Cohen, Edwin S., 130, 192

INDEX

collective bargaining and pension plans, 15, 16, 17, 81
College Retirement Equities Fund (CREF), 82
Collier, Harold R., 157
Colorado, 31
communications industry and pension plans, 94
conflicts of interest and pension plans, 72–3, 77, 104–6, 113
Congress, U.S., 1, 100, 108, 120, 123, 126, 127, 128, 152, 159, 163, 194
Consolidated Food Corporation, 52, 53
construction industry and pension plans, 6, 94
Continental Illinois National Bank and Trust Company, 105
Copeland, Lamont du Pont, Jr., 67
cost-of-living formulas of some pension plans, 82, 119, 140, 166
craft and railroad union pension funds, 14
credited service, complicated ways of counting, 38, 43
Curtis, Carl T., 155
Curtiss Wright: Electronics Division, 83; Engine Division, 83–4

Daly, Ed, 135, 192
Daniels, Wilbur: on ILGWU retirement fund, 129–30
Davis, Frank: on layoffs, job changes, and pension benefits, 83–4
Day, Ann: on layoffs and pension requirements, 35
D.C. Transit Company, 72
death benefits: *see* survivors' benefits
Defense, U.S. Department of, 134–5, 169 and passim
defense industry and job and pension security, 134, 169–78
deferred wages vs. gratuities concept of private pensions, 17
Dent, John H., 108, 156, 194; on conglomerates, layoffs, and pension funds, 53

Dent bill, 109, 110, 111, 112, 113, 114, 115, 116
de Paola, Joseph, 67
Detroit Gasket and Manufacturing Company, 39–40
Detroit-Packard plant, 50
Dingell, John, 157
disability, and pension plans, 7, 23, 80
discharge as a means to avoid paying pensions, 35–6
discrimination, and pension plans: against minorities, 84; against women, 84–6; against lower-wage employees, 84, 88, 90, 133; "permissible," 88–9

early retirement payments, amount of, 80, 89–90
Eastern Conference of Health, Welfare and Pension Plans, 195
Eaton Company, 71
economic power of private pension funds, 103–4
economy, the, business, and pensions, 45–56
Eddystone, Pennsylvania, 45, 46
Edwards, Roy V., 86
Ehrlinger, Robert John, 169–78
E. I. duPont de Nemours & Company, 67
eligibility rules for pensions, 4–5, 8, 30–44, 139–41, 160, 189–90; years of service, 32–3, 34, 38, 43; age requirement, 32–3, 34, 37, 43; employment under plan at time of retirement, 32, 140; continuous service requirement, 34–5, 42, 46–7, 110; change of jobs, 36–7; employment with a competitor forbidden, 38–9; retired workers may not work in industry, 39; procedures that must be followed, 39–40; proposed removal of all restrictive, 116
Employee Benefits Protection Act, 113
employer-financed pension plans: *see* private pension system
equity annuity plans, 82, 140
Erlenborn, John N., 108, 156

INDEX 211

executives, retirement benefits received by top, 86

F-105 bomber cutback, 49
F-111 contract, 48, 171
Fairchild-Stratos Corporation, 48, 171
federal government: and programs to provide economic security in old age, 2–3; pension legislation and, 11, 62, 108–26, 130–1, 154–7; nonintervention in pension-loss cases, 40–1; and insurance for pension funds, 61; action in cases of fund abuse, 66; regulation of pension funds, need for, 131–2
fiduciary rules to hold pension fund trustees accountable, proposed, 113–15, 157
Flanigan, Peter M., 191
Florida, 37, 48
Flowers, Stanley: on Teamster Union practices in denying pension benefits, 41
Ford Instrument Company, 48
Ford Motor Company, 86
Friedrich, Otto: on *Saturday Evening Post*, 52–3
funded pension plans, 25, 29; proposals for ensuring, 111–12, 117, 121, 157, 160
FXR, 48

General Mills Corporation, 86
General Motors Corporation, 86
General Telephone Company of Kentucky, 35
Genesco Company, 72
Gojmerac, John, 57–8, 63
Goodman, Isidore, 133, 192
graded vesting, 109; *see also* vesting
"grandfather" provision of Williams-Javits bill, 116–17
Granite Cutters retirement fund, 14
Greyhound Corporation, 46
Griffin, Robert P., 155
Griffiths, Martha W.: on who receives pension benefits, 103
Griggs, Cooper & Company, 52

group life insurance provided by some companies, 99–100
Grumman Aerospace, 48, 171

Halpern, Seymour, 157
Harper's magazine, 52
Hartke, Vance, 155
Hat Trimmers Union Local 7 Retirement Fund, 58
Haws Refractories, 57
Health, Education and Welfare, U.S. Department of, 157, 193
Helstoski, Henry, 157
Hodgson, James, 179, 180, 191; on funding, 121
Honeywell Corporation, 170
Hotel & Restaurant Employees and Bartenders International Union, 74–5
House Banking and Currency Committee, 106
House Education and Labor Committee, 156, 157
House General Subcommittee on Labor, 70, 149, 156
House Ways and Means Committee, 108, 130, 156, 157

Iacocca, Lee, 86
improving the private pension system, what you can do toward: support national private pension legislation, 127–33; help influence employers and union officials, 127, 137–8, 139; where to get information and what you want to know, 179–90, 191–7; organize to change your pension plan, 141–7, 161–2
individual annual investments for personal pension program, proposed, 115, 121–2, 155, 156
Inland Steel Supreme Court decision (1949), 16
Institutional Investor, 78
insurance companies' handling of pension funds, 75–6
insured pension plans, 25, 29; *see also* reinsurance

"integration" method of computing benefits, 86–8, 87 n.
"interlocking directorships," 105–6
Internal Revenue Code, 50
Internal Revenue Service (I.R.S.), 9, 21, 24, 26, 53, 54, 58–9, 59 n., 87–8, 90, 116, 118, 119–20, 133, 192
International Brotherhood of Electrical Workers, 56
International Brotherhood of Teamsters: *see* Teamsters Union
International Harvester Company, 51
International Ladies' Garment Workers Union, 56, 129–30
International Telephone & Telegraph, 83
investments, poor, as threat to pension funds, 75–8 and passim
Investors Diversified Services, 105
Investors Mutual, Inc., 105

Jalmer, Peter: on plant closing and loss of pension, 45–6
Jamieson, J. K., 86
Javits, Jacob, 56, 108, 109, 116, 117, 120, 134, 154, 155, 160; on private pension funds, 3, 5
Johnstown, Pennsylvania, 57
Joint Economic Committee, 100, 101
Jones & Laughlin Steel Corporation, 4
Journeymen Barbers, Hairdressers, Cosmetologists and Proprietors' International Union, 66, 68
Justice, U.S. Department of, 69, 135, 193

Kendall Company, 90
Kirk, Ken W., 40
Kleiler, Frank M., 192
Kolodrubetz, Walter W., 193
Kropp Forge Company Employee Savings and Profit Sharing Fund, 73

Labor, U.S. Department of, 10, 40, 43, 66, 68, 73, 112, 116, 120, 132–4, 135, 138, 156, 159, 179, 180 and passim, 191
labor unions: *see* unions

lack of credits as reason for forfeit of pension, 30–1, 43
Laird, Melvin R., 169
Lakewood, California, 6
Landay, Donald M., 192
Las Vegas, 69
layoffs and pension plans, 7, 11, 31, 33, 34, 35, 43, 47, 48–50, 51, 52–6, 80, 84
Leary, Joseph P., 195
Ledbetter, Donald L., 169–78
legislation, pension, 11, 62, 108–26, 128, 129, 154–7, 159–61
Levenson, Alan B., 193
Lexington, Kentucky, 35
Life Insurance Association of America, 161
Lineberger, Frank: on General Telephone Company, 35
Ling-Temco-Vought (LTV), 86
lobbying of pension industry by beneficiaries, proposed, 123–4, 133
Lockheed, 19
Long, Russell B., 155, 194
Long Island, 49
Los Angeles, 48
Lurie, Leonard J., 133, 192

McClung, Nelson, 100
McFarland, James P., 86
McGill, Dan: on private pension plans, 2–3
McGrory Corporation, 73
McNealus, Arthur L., 48, 169–78
Master Mates & Pilots Union, 36
Memphis, Tennessee, 39
mergers, transfers, and pension plans, 48, 50–2
Midwest Pension Conference, 128, 196
Miller, Edward B., 193
Mills, Wilbur, 108, 156, 194
miners and the pension system, 4–5, 41–2, 131, 136
Minnesota Supreme Court, 53
Mintz, Joseph, 6–7
misuse and mismanagement of pension funds, 52–5, 65–78, 135
Monthly Labor Review, 47

INDEX

Morgan Guaranty Trust Company, 105
mortality and pension plans, 23, 96–7, 140
multiemployer pension plans, 16–17, 32, 36, 37, 55, 118–19, 140

Nader, Ralph, 126, 134, 152, 158, 179, 180
National Association of Manufacturers, 128, 161, 196
National Bank of Washington, 70
National Council of Senior Citizens, 145, 196
National Foundation of Health, Welfare and Pension Plans, 74–5, 128, 196
National Gypsum Company, 170
National Labor Relations Board (NLRB), 16, 136, 193
National Retired Teachers Association, 196
National Senior Citizens Law Center, 137
National Society of Professional Engineers Pension Study Group, 196
New Hampshire, 42
New York Hotel Trades Council Pension Fund, 60–1
New York State Insurance Department, 58
Newark, New Jersey, 121
Newport, Oregon, 36
Nixon, Richard M., 108, 110, 111, 112, 113, 116, 122, 130, 155, 159, 191
Nixon bill ("rule of fifty"; H.R. 12272), 120–2, 156, 159
noninsured pension plans, 25, 76–7
North Kingstown, Rhode Island, 131

Oakes, Harry, 7
odds on collecting a pension, 5–6
Office of Economic Opportunity (OEO), 136, 137
O'Hara, Robert P.: on loss of pension due to application paper loss, 39–40
Ohio, 37

old age income assurance proposals, 2–3, 100
Old Age Survivors Insurance: *see* Social Security
operating costs of pension plans, 23

Packard Company, 51
Painters Pension Fund of Suffolk County, 74
"partial terminations," 118; *see also* business shutdowns
"past service credits," 26–7
Patman, Wright: on Penn Central stock sales, 106
Penn Central, 105–6
Pennsylvania, 5
Pension Research Council, 196
Pensions and Severance Pay for Displaced Defense Workers (Folk), 172
personal savings as a source of retirement income, 93, 101, 102, 155, 156
Peyser, Peter A., 156
Pfizer Drugs, 86
portability, 110–11, 155, 157; *see also* vesting
Powers, John J., Jr., 86
President's Committee on Corporate Pension Funds (1965), 100
President's Task Force on Aging (1970), 100
private pension system, 1–3; and the promise to pay, 4–11; stakes in, 12–18; how pensions work, 19–29; eligibility rules for collecting under, 30–44; effect of the economy on, 45–56; termination of benefits due to lack of funds, 57–61; insuring, 61–3; management and mismanagement of pension funds, 65–78; how much a person will collect under, 79–91; and the public stake in how well it covers retired workers and their families, 92–107; proposed reforms of, 108–26; what individuals can do to improve, 127–47
Prudence Mutual Casualty Company, 67

questionnaire, pension, and its findings, 149–53

Reed, Charlie, 4–5
reforms of pension system, proposed, 17, 73, 108–26, 154–7, 159–61; *see also under specific proposals*
reinsurance of private pension plans, proposed, 61–2, 112–13, 119, 155, 156
relocation of company, and pension plans, 46
Republic Aviation Company, 49–50
retirement benefits received under private pensions, 79–91, 92–102
Richfield, Ohio, 41
right to know about your pension plan, your legal, 138–9
Roche, James, 86
Rodino, Peter W., 156
Romnes, H. I., 86
Ruff, Charles, 135, 193
"rule of fifty," Nixon, 110, 120–1, 130
Ryan Aviation, 88

St. Louis, 47
St. Paul, 7
Salem, New Jersey, 7
San Diego, 55
Sanders, Edgar, 66
Santa Barbara, 47
Santa Cruz, 47
Saturday Evening Post, 52–3
Saunders, Stuart, 105
Schulz, James: on death benefits, 99
Seafarers International Union, 36
Sears, Roebuck & Company, 72
seasonal worker, problems of the, 117
Securities and Exchange Commission, 120, 125, 163, 193
Segall, Joel, 192
Self-Employed Retirement Act (1963), 96
self-employed tax-deductible investments for pension savings, 115–16
service industry and pension plans, 94, 95

Senate Committee on Finance, 155, 156, 194
Senate Committee on Labor and Public Welfare, 155, 194
Senate Labor Subcommittee, 60, 79–80, 89, 90, 121, 149, 194
Senate Special Committee on Aging, 59 n.
Shaheen, Thomas A., 66–7
Sheehan, Jack, 197
Shore, B. C.: on loss of pension money due to refusal to transfer credits, 36
Shultz, George P.: on pension fund loss and mismanagement, 10, 70
Silberman, Laurence H., 191
single-employer pension plans, 32–3, 35–6
Sixth Annual Conference on Employee Benefits (1972), 126
small businesses and pension plans, 95–6
Social Security Act of 1935, 15, 157
Social Security Administration, 193
Social Security benefits, 13, 15, 16, 21–2, 47, 79–80, 85 n., 86–7, 90–92, 93, 96, 100, 101, 106–7, 122–3, 126, 166, 168
Solo Cup Company, 72
South Bend, Indiana, 9
Southern Pension Conference, 128, 197
Space Technology Laboratories, 48, 171
Spica, Vincent V., 39, 40
Standard Oil Company, Inc., 86
Steel Industry Fact Finding Committee, 16
steel industry pension plans, 34
Strategic Air Command Communication System, 83
Studebaker-Packard Corporation, 51, 60, 119
Studebaker plant closing, 9
Supreme Court, U.S., 16, 81, 85
survivors' benefits under private pension plans, 96–101, 117, 140, 142, 143–4, 156–7, 158, 160
Sweeney, David A., 196

INDEX

tax deferrals for personal retirement program of individuals, proposed, 115, 121–2, 160
tax incentive to private pension system, 3, 9, 15, 21–2, 62, 88–9, 95–6, 102–3, 158
Teachers Insurance and Annuity Association (TIAA), 56, 82, 197
Teamsters Union, 17, 36, 196; Local 407 (Cleveland), 41; Central States Pension Fund, 36, 41, 68–9
termination of pension funds due to lack of money, 57–61
Thayer, Paul, 86
Treasury, U.S. Department of the, 73, 112, 119, 130, 155, 192
trustee: job of pension, 25–6, 29; misuse of funds by, 74–5
Tyler, James, 6
Tyson, Robert C.: on mandatory funding requirements, 129

"underfunding" of pension plans, 9, 60, 63
"unfunded" pension plans, 24–5
unions and union pension plans, 1, 5, 6, 8, 9, 10, 13–18, 19–24, 33, 38, 41, 43, 46, 47–8, 55–6, 58, 62, 63, 70–1, 94, 117, 122, 123, 127, 128, 129–30, 140; *see also entries on specific unions*
Uniroyal, Inc., 60
United Aircraft Corporation, 48, 171
United Auto Workers Union, 16, 55, 59–60, 61, 96, 98–9, 100, 128, 197
United Mine Workers Union, 17–18, 56; Welfare and Retirement Fund, 41–2, 70–1, 131
U.S. Arms Control and Disarmament Agency, 49
U.S. Chamber of Commerce, 128, 129, 161
U.S. District Court for the District of Columbia, 70–1
United States Retirement Plan Bonds, 170, 176, 177
United States Steel Corporation, 129
United Steelworkers Union, 16, 55, 61, 62, 128, 197

Universal Cyclops Steel Company, 37
Usery, W. J., 138, 192

vested rights and liabilities, 33–4, 37, 38, 39, 44, 48, 49, 51, 53, 54, 55, 60–1, 62, 63, 64, 83, 90, 109–10, 112, 114, 117, 118–19, 120, 121, 133, 139–40, 141–2, 149–50, 155, 156, 159, 160

Welfare and Pension Plans Disclosure Act, 66, 69–70, 159, 179
welfare programs for the elderly, 92, 106
West Kentucky Coal Company, 71
Western Conference of Teamsters, 5
Western Pension Conference, 128, 197
Western Union Telegraph Company, 60
Westinghouse Atomic Power, 170
Westinghouse Electrical Corporation, 171
White House Conference on Aging (1971), 100, 159
wholesale and retail trades and pension plans, 94
widows, and how they fare under pension plans, 13, 96–100, 117, 143, 158, 160
Williams, Harrison A., Jr., 56, 108, 154, 160, 194; on closing of Ballantine Brewery, 121
Williams-Javits bill, 109–12, 113, 114, 116, 117, 118–19, 130, 154–5, 160
Williamsville, New York, 35
Wilson & Company, Inc., 86
Winn-Dixie Corporation, 72–3
Winthrop Lawrence Corporation, 67
Wojnarowski, Joseph, 57–8
women: Social Security benefits received by, 79, 85 n.; pension benefits and discrimination against, 84–6, 96; and Williams-Javits bill, 117–18
Woodcock, Leonard: on public reinsurance of private pension plans, 61
Woodlynn, New Jersey, 45